Lost & Found

Personal Story Publishing Project Series

Bearing Up , 2018
- making do, bearing up, and overcoming adversity

Exploring , 2019
- discoveries, challenges, and adventures

That Southern Thing , 2020
- living, loving, laughing, loathing, leaving the South

Luck and Opportunity , sping 2021
- between if and if only

Trouble , fall 2021
- causing, avoiding, getting in, and getting out

Curious Stuff , spring 2022
- mementos, treasures, white elephants, and junk

Twists and Turns, fall 2022
- inflection points in life by choice, happenstance, misfortune, failure, and grace

Available through Daniel Boone Footsteps
www.danielboonefootsteps.com
www.RandellJones.com
1959 N. Peace Haven Rd., #105
Winston-Salem, NC 27106

Lost & Found

Randell Jones, editor

Daniel Boone Footsteps
Winston-Salem, North Carolina

Daniel Boone Footsteps
1959 N. Peace Haven Rd., #105
Winston-Salem, NC 27106

RandellJones.com
DanielBooneFootsteps.com
DBooneFootsteps@gmail.com

Parting is all we know of heaven,
And all we need of hell."
—Emily Dickinson

Preface

This book is the eightth in a series of anthologies, collections of personal stories on a set theme, our Personal Story Publishing Project. Since beginning in 2018, our collections have included the themes:
Bearing Up, "making do, bearing up, and overcoming adversity,"
Exploring, "discoveries, challenges, and adventure."
That Southern Thing, "living, loving, laughing, loathing, leaving the South."
Luck and Opportunity, "between if and if only"
Trouble, "causing, avoiding, getting in, and getting out,"
Curious Stuff, "mementos, treasures, white elephants, and junk,."
and *Twists and Turns*, "inflection points in life by choice, happenstance, misfortune, failure, and grace."

The book you are holding is the result of our eighth Call for Personal Stories, this one on the theme: "Lost & Found—loss and discovery—trials, serendipity, and after." We thank the scores of writers who responded to the call by submitting such interesting, thoughtful, and well-crafted stories. They delivered the diversity and depth of perspective we were hoping for and the insight to self which proved we chose the right theme. Each story is targeted between 750 and 800 words, so the writers were challenged in executing their craft, telling an interesting story succinctly. The writers and we have all found the Personal Story Publishing Project through its eight iterations, so far, to be an instructive and rewarding writing experience. For the readers, it is a delight.

We received submissions from many writers in North Carolina and across the South, notably, but also from writers reaching across the country from Florida to the West Coast including Kentucky, Texas, Arizona, Pennsylvania, Illinois, and Canada. We wish we could have printed them all, but we are delighted to continue curating 45 stories for each collection.

In June 2019, we launched a second outlet for sharing the work of these fine writers with a broader audience. Their work can now be heard in our twice weekly podcast, "6-minute Stories." Our podcast is available through Apple Podcasts (iTunes), Spotify, and Stitcher. You can listen directly to "6-minute Stories" and find all the stories archived at RandellJones.com/6minutestories. Episodes are announced on Facebook @6minutestories.

Lost & Found, the Personal Story Publishing Project, and "6-minute Stories" podcast are undertaken by author and publisher Randell Jones, doing business as Daniel Boone Footsteps in Winston-Salem, North Carolina.

Thank you for enjoying and appreciating good storytelling. And, remember . . .
    Everybody loves a good story.[sm] •

Contents

Preface   vii
Contents   ix-xiv
Introduction   xv

Instincts   1
   by Marci Spencer, Old Fort, NC
    — The hawk had never seen such a wild creature!

If Only …   5
   by Erika Hoffman, Chapel Hill, NC
    — I have loved you dearly.

Letting the Bunny Go   9
   by B.E. Jackson, Skull Valley, AZ
    — smelling the verdant breath of spring

In Search of Solace   13
   by Claudia Chowaniec, Ottawa, Ontario, Canada
    — I have made it to here.

Signature, Please   17
   by Annette L. Brown, Atwater, CA
    — "And you're sassy, too!"

Handful of Gravel   21
   by Wendy Jett, Lexington, KY
    — a poisonous snake searching for prey

A Voice Lost ... and Found   25
        by Richard L. Davis, Augusta, GA
        — Treasure in hand, I felt like an intruder.

Gold Star Mothers   29
        by Thomas Gery, Reading, PA
        — an award no one wants

The Drive   33
        by Lucinda Trew, Charlotte, NC
        — We are together, on a lovely, meandering road.

Oh, Brother   37
        by Stephanie Dean, Mocksville, NC
        — a repetitious exercise of accusations and denials

The Lost Spaceship   41
        by Donald Cartwright, Winnetka, IL
        — rocket man

It's Not the Pearls   45
        by Emily Rosen, Boca Raton, FL
        — I had also lost that "other me."

In the Heart of Trauma   49
         by Arlene Mandell, Linville, NC
        — This became my strategy—and my problem.

The Worst Day of My Life   53
        by John S. Viccellio, Matthews, NC
        — I was mortified. I was 9 years old.

Black Dome Reprise   57
    by Kenneth Chamlee, Mills River, NC
    – our upward toil over sharp rocks, deadfall, and slippery moss

The Tall and Caring Man   61
    by Lisa Williams Kline, Davidson, NC
    – from a grateful mother's heart

Deathbed Promise   65
    by Linda Vigen Phillips, Charlotte, NC
    – No family is left to fact-check the story.

One Soul Alone   69
    by Janet K. Baxter, Kings Mountain, NC
    – How long are you going to be unhappy?

Taking Flight   73
    by Akira Odani, St. Augustine, FL
    – like a soaring hawk

The Gift   77
    by Cherie Cox, Charlotte, NC
    – You changed my life.

Pop the Kettle On   81
    by Rose-Mary Harrington, Wilmington, NC
    – resolved with a cup of tea

In Transition   85
    by Jane Satchell McAllister, Mocksville, NC
    – Falling Tree pose anyone?

Contents

xi

The Application   89
     by Landis Wade, Charlotte, NC
     — Once you're in, you have to apply to get out.

My Father's Photograph   93
     by Bob Amason, St. Augustine, FL
     — frozen in time—hope, optimism, joy

The Sound of Music   97
     by Alexandra Goodwin, Coral Springs, FL
     — What a Wonderful World

Alone in the Woods   101
     by Suzanne Cottrell, Oxford, NC
     — A toddler's missing. Can you help?

The Mezuzah   105
     by Ginny Foard, Sullivan's Island, SC
     — a prayer, a gathering, a blessing

Finding the Perfect Pumpkin   109
     by Rebecca S. Holder, Winston-Salem, NC
     — She was a hugger.

Six Minutes to You   113
     by David Inserra, Hilton Head Island, SC
     — Ten women. Six minutes at a time.

Finding Joy in Borrowed Time   117
     by Patricia Joslin, Charlotte, NC
     — much more kind and clever

Holding Hands 121
    by Karen Sleeth, Durham, NC
      — *"I don't want you to get lost."*

Tea with the Queen 125
    by Kay Harper Windsor, Winston-Salem, NC
      — *spirited curiosity and spunk*

A Fine Work 129
    by Joe Brown, Bethania, NC
      — *Mom's busy hands*

Love Never Dies 133
    by Phyllis Castelli, Henderson, NC
      — *an angel of compassion*

Up the Creek 137
    by Howard Pearre, Winston-Salem, NC
      — *We had lost our paddles.*

The Blessings of Unanswered Prayers 141
    by Gene Hoots, Charlotte, NC
      — *All the "experts" were wrong.*

The Essentials 145
    by Catherine Parisio, West Linn, OR
      — *How could we have been so stupid?*

Historic Preservation Goes off the Rails 149
    by Harry Enoch, Winchester, KY
      — *The project suffered one disaster after another.*

Contents

Blue Light Blues   153
     by Patricia E. Watts, Mountville, SC
     — I don't think the judge knew quite what to do with me.

Finding Home   157
     by J.P. McGillicuddy, Charlotte, NC
     — My life had ricocheted in unpredictable directions.

A Terrible Way To Live   161
     by Phyliss Grady Adcock, Morehead City, NC
     — The bride is no longer naïve.

Tough Times   165
     by Paula Teem Levi, Clover, SC
     — "I out-foxed those fellers."

Uplifting Good Fortune   169
     by Judie Holcomb-Pack, Winston-Salem, NC
     — What we never considered was aerodynamics.

GPS on the Blue Ridge Parkway   173
     by David Winship, Bristol, TN
     — On we drove, mile by mile, searching through the heavy fog.

It Was Not Her Fault   177
     by Randell Jones, Winston-Salem, NC
     — somebody wanted a pound of flesh

Introduction

"Lost and Found." The two words together most often take us back to our childhood school days when, if we were lucky, we were immersed in a nurturing system that seemed designed to get us back home with everything we had brought in. Not so later on. We soon discovered that life chips away in little nips and bites and sometimes in whole swipes and gulps at our underpinnings, our beliefs about ourselves, our expectations, our dreams, and the people, creatures, and things we love. We don't, in fact, in life always get home with everything we hoped to.

Lost is a heavy word; it's serious business. It suggests separation and distress, and it has a ring of finality that grabs our attention immediately. Found is a lighter, more encouraging word, offering up serendipity and visions of a new beginning, a restoration, a salvation, a grace.

But losing something we did not want can be a blessing, and finding out something we did not want to know can be a curse. So, these words have meanings we create for ourselves, each of our lives alone offering up sometimes muted, perhaps surreptitious, definitions.

Lost and Found can be circular, also, each leading to the other. Lost can be a moment of stunned awareness of something missing, something gone. Found can be a hallelujah moment of victory and recovery. Either can create a moment of reckoning, a settling, an acceptance, a coming to terms with change—perhaps change we did not invite, did not expect, did not want, but change nonetheless. In time, we may discover that *we* have changed, and the world looks different to us. We know things we did not know before. The world surprises us again, and we surprise ourselves, again. We discover that we have come full circle. In the loss, we find ourselves bereft, diminished. In the finding, we lose the dread, the anxiety, the fear that took us into our own moments or passages of distress and despair, moments that took us to a sense of loss for a while—for as long as it took us to find our way out. Circular indeed.

We are gratified by the response to our eighth Call for Personal Stories, and we are grateful to all the writers who invested time and energy into crafting personal stories for possible inclusion in this anthology. From among the submissions, we chose stories to include based on the quality of the writing and the resonance of the personal experiences shared with the announced theme, "Lost & Found—personal stories of loss and discovery—trials, serendipity, and life after."

We have stories of finding courage: a young girl shows bravery beyond her years, protecting those in her care; another defends herself in a vicious attack after suffering at the hands of those she thought friends; and, a young woman finds the right mindset for dealing with a wrong-headed jerk.

We have stories of seeking: searching for the journals hidden away, the only stories that matter anymore; finding the peace, at last, to reach out and to listen with kindness and care in amends for a youthful spurning; savoring time with Mother along the backroads of memories and across the countryside of love; and, recovering the voice that was there all along.

We have stories of discovery: the perils of pearls and the club life to living authentically; the bother in the brother; that the trials of the trail get thicker and darker for foolhardy hikers; that a bedroom door that locked was the key to her deepest adolescent fears; and, the face you've never seen in the person you've always known.

We have stories of love: a mother's love alone is not enough to make a child happy; even a son at the top of his class cannot top a father's unconditional love; and, making space in your heart for a dog will eventually become a hole you fill with another helping of love.

We have stories of being struck with dread: a mortal fear of the teacher creates a puddle of problems for a young boy; the height of a mother's fears is shortened by a smiling child perched atop a towering stroller; and, a river of over-confidence is dashed against the perilous rocks of real danger.

We have stories of reckoning with the future: aging into gratitude; finagling a future free from the courtroom; taking the slow road to love in the fast-paced world of speed dating; and, still dreaming of space adventures launched from a gumball machine.

We have stories offering advice: teatime is story time; searching for the lost is more stressful than it looks; Big Friendly Giants bring queen-sized dreams; and, more than just the roof can collapse when restoring old buildings.

These are some of the stories among all those we share in this collection. We think our writers have brought their best for you to read, to consider, and to reflect on. And whatever time and energy you bring to reading and rereading this collection, we hope you find yourself changed for the better in your life afterward by these writers' trials and serendipities.

We also hope you get home with everything you brought. If not, you might check the Lost & Found. •

RJ

Instincts
by Marci Spencer

Brooke's life had changed. Her dad's drinking habits forced her and her mom to move to a safer home. My once-bubbly granddaughter entered the first grade withdrawn, lost, and confused. She fell prey to classroom harassment.

We talked about the mean jokes at school. I thought I offered empathetic words, but I guess not. My intentions were good but misunderstood. She thought that I'd been around so long that I'd forgotten how hard it was to be a kid. We separated to busy ourselves while we thought about things.

I weeded the garden. Brooke cleaned the homing pigeon loft. She'd helped me tend the white doves many times when we'd catch them before a training session or ceremonial release. They'd circle a wedding or special event as a symbol of hope and peace, like the doves at the Olympics, then fly home.

Brooke placed the doves on the platform outside the window to exercise in the sun while she cleaned the rows of nesting boxes. She gently netted each one as it lifted from its perch, raining a flurry of white feathers. Scoop, net, release, scrape; scoop another, net again, release outside, scrape some more.

She developed a rhythm.

Absorbed in her duties, Brooke was unaware that a Sharp-shinned Hawk, with its long, narrow wings, banked around tree branches and headed toward the loft. Homers strutted on the rooftop after exercise-loops over the pond. Some preened; others rested. As the hawk dropped in for the kill, his quarry burst into flight as one mass flock. Downy white feathers dusted the air.

The hawk singled out his target, lowered his talons, and pinned his victim to the ground.

"Leave my birds alone!" shrieked Brooke. "Get out of here! Find your dinner somewhere else!" Unsure of his own safety, the startled hawk left as fast as he came. Those doves were under her care, and she was not going to let them get hurt. The hawk, however, was not giving up easily.

The lone dove, dazed but not injured, rejoined the flock. The confused birds flew in loose, uncoordinated circles, but their instinct was to fly home to their safehouse with its food and shelter. Pairs of tiny feet lowered onto the loft roof while the hawk scouted out his next move from a nearby poplar tree. Bright-white, easy-to-see "fast-food" dinners were within his reach. After migrating south ahead of winter winds, he was hungry.

"Get in the loft, guys!" Brooke pleaded. "Go inside where he can't get you." She wanted them to enter the window like they always did after a long flight. Don't dally! Not today! But they sat frozen in fear, clinging to the edge of their roof.

With high-pitched calls—sounding like "Kill! Kill! Kill!"—the hawk advanced. Two quick wingbeats pumped before easing into a glide. Two more crisp wingbeats, then a glide moved him closer. Two more, a glide; two more, a glide. The hawk was confident in his plan but so was Brooke.

She planted her feet and screamed as he narrowed the distance. As the hawk entered his dive, she hurled inner tubes, insect repellant cans, and tennis balls, left after the summer's fun.

The hawk had never seen such a wild creature! He veered off, returning to his lofty vantage point. Twice more, announcing his entry with intense cries, the hawk attempted his attack and dodged torpedo life jackets, oars, and water bottles. Hawk and girl squared off; he closer to heaven with perfect eyesight, and she, guarding her Flight Team, lined up shoulder-to-shoulder, with lakeshore oddities.

She faced their enemy like a leader on a battlefield. Wild commotion broke the silence behind her. Turning around, she saw the whole flock flying right at her. A second hawk had attacked from the rear!

"How dare you!" shouted Brooke. Like a beaver flapping his wide tail in alarm, she raised an oar and smacked it hard on the surface of the pond. A cannon had fired on the battlefield!

Hawk #2 flew west. Hawk #1 also left, flying who-knows-where. The scattered doves gradually landed on the windowsill and re-entered their clean loft. They were safe at home, protected by a little-girl-sergeant ready to defend their Alamo.

I had heard the commotion. Naturally, my grand-maternal instincts urged me to run and help Brooke with her battle. But

Instincts

she seemed confident, determined. My heart whispered to my soul, "That's my girl!"

"Is everything all right, Honey?" I asked, approaching from the garden.

Brooke hummed a tune while she finished dusting off duff and dander from the nesting boxes.

I'm almost finished," she said.

"Feeling better?"

"You know, Nona?" she said. "Sometimes you just gotta face your problems. Stay cool and stand strong. And when others depend on you, you have to believe in yourself."

Protective instincts, it seems, helped Brooke find her inner strength and self-confidence again—more effective, I suppose, than any words of wisdom from someone who had been around so long. •

A native of Asheville, North Carolina, now living in Old Fort, Marci Spencer grew up on land that her great-grandfather refused to sell to George Vanderbilt for the Biltmore Estate. She worked as a nurse practitioner in the fields of cardiology, family medicine, and overseas medical missionary service. After hiking hundreds of miles, volunteering for the park service, and earning certification as a naturalist/environmental educator, Marci wrote *Clingmans Dome, Highest Mountain in the Great Smokies*; *Pisgah National Forest: a History*; *Nantahala National Forest: a History*; and, *Pisgah Inn*—all published by Arcadia/History Press.

If Only ...
by Erika Hoffman

If only I were a poet, I'd compose lines, like John Greenleaf Whittier. In a few couplets, I could set down for eternity how I feel. That would be a relief. Longform writing seldom captures the sharp edges of grief. Poems do. Who wants to wind on and on about one's personal sadness? I wish I had a metaphor to share like the one in *Telling the Bees*, the black cloth draped over hives. I need something to alert to avert. Perhaps, I should don a small dark carnation to warn and ward off folks. It would convey I was not in the mood for small talk or light-hearted banter. Often, people don't know how to react to someone mourning. They don't know what to say. So, they avoid the subject. In old European countries, people wore black for days, weeks, months. But not now. Now no one wears mourning dresses every day, like Queen Victoria who grieved her Albert's death for decades. Outwardly, in current society you look the same; you dress the same as before your heart was shredded.

I'm not sad about a life I knew, a friendship I had, of things past never to come again. I cannot gaze at a photo and remember good times. I cannot immerse myself in memories.

My grief differs. I'm sad about the future. I wanted this grand-daughter. It's not because I don't have grandchildren. I am blessed with them. I have much to be thankful for. I know what a baby means. I wanted this one too.

Had she been lost early before completely formed, I could sigh and say, "nature's way." But she was a fully rounded baby one could cradle. She was a beauty with fingernails, and long dark eyelashes, and jet-black hair, and chubby thighs that I could hold and pretend she is only asleep. She was like a sleeping Cleopatra. If only she could awaken, then my daughter and son-in-law and all of us would rouse from this horrible nightmare and clutch her tightly. Could we turn back the clock? Just a couple of days. Let's reset to when there was a vivid heartbeat in her little chest, a visible pulsating heart. If only she had been birthed two weeks before her due date.

I research "stillborn babies." Alcohol consumption, smoking, drugs, too young a mom, too old a mom, no pre-natal visits, bad nutrition, infection, accidents—these things can cause a child never to be born alive. My daughter was healthy, educated, saw the ob-gyn regularly, did not smoke or drink, was not sick, was vaccinated against Covid, did not have an accident, was not too young or too old and had given birth twice before. *What went wrong?*

The day it happened was the day Russia invaded Ukraine. Many tragedies occur that aren't preventable; why would anyone purposely inflict pain? On TV, I see the Ukrainian babies and their moms running. *Why is this happening?*

Time goes on. Tragedies continue. Preventable ones.

I will comfort my daughter, seeking words that do and avoiding words that inflict any preventable sadness. I ask my daughter no questions. I ask myself only those spinning-hamster-wheel questions I have.

Why are you gone, Lili Ana? Why couldn't I have met you? Why can't I be a poet to express my heartbreak? I see the hospital photograph, black and white, of you with your curled left hand around your mom's finger as your clenched fist is touching your cheek as if you are pondering a question.

"For you are beautiful and I have loved you dearly, more dearly than the spoken word can tell" are lyrics from a song sung by an English sailor going off to fight a war. Yet, when I heard them sung today on an old recording of *Farewell*, I thought how eerily true they are of all grief.

Why do devastating things happen you never see coming? You wake up one morning naïve and gullible thinking this day will be like the day before; you look forward to what lies ahead in the immediate future, and *wham*, the phone rings and the spinning world has changed. It's come to a screeching halt. A lump sticks in my throat. I am disoriented. I am confused.

I cannot compose a poem. I can pen my feelings merely in simple longhand. I do not tell bees of the death of my grandbaby. I sit alone here in my study and cry to my dachs-hunds at my feet. One was my daughter's dog long ago. She

If Only …

looks at me with sad eyes. I am no poet, yet this doggie seems to understand, although I have no verses to recite. How to relate the sadly unrelatable? The sensory language poets use is needed. I am no poet. Just a heartbroken grandma.

If only ... •

Erika Hoffman of Chatham County, North Carolina, has been writing with the goal of publication for 12 years. She's been published 430 times in venues such as anthologies, newspapers, magazines, and ezines. Her niche is the non-fiction narrative although she has written novels. Erika received her undergraduate and graduate degrees from Duke University where she met her husband. Besides teaching high school, Erika kept busy raising four children. She belongs to a few writing groups: NC Writers Network, Carteret Writers, and TAF.

Letting the Bunny Go
by B.E. Jackson

A scratching sound in the hay barn greeted my nightly trip to feed the horses. When I aimed my flashlight at the noise, I saw a small, wriggling, white cotton ball tucked into the far corner. It was the back end of the world's tiniest cottontail rabbit, and I was standing between it and freedom.

A pair of barn cats were eyeing the bunny with interest, so I did what any self-respecting animal lover would do. I gently scooped up the trembling animal in the yogurt cup I used to measure grain. At the house I scanned the bookshelves, found my copy of *A Field Guide to Mammals*, and turned to the section marked Rabbits and read:

> *The cottontail rabbit is not only undomesticated, it is of a different genus than the European-descended domestic rabbit.*

I might have easily lived my entire life without discovering that *Sylvilagus* (cottontail) does not equal *Oryctolagus* (domestic) on a genetic level.

Used to thigh-high and taller pets, I had no idea what to feed this tiny creature. Back to the field guide I went:

> *Dandelion greens and hay (timothy and oat hay) are extremely important for wild rabbits. As soon as their eyes are open, you may also introduce the bunnies to alfalfa pellets.*

I lined a cardboard box with alfalfa pellets and timothy hay, filled measuring cups with water and a few plucked dandelions, and marveled at how, really, a bunny was a cheap pet for people who don't weed their lawns and have horse feed on hand.

The next day, a short trip to Petco changed all that. I strolled down multiple aisles of cages, waterers, feeders, athletic equipment (to keep your rodent fit), and rodent toys to prevent boredom. In the end, I walked out with a modestly priced cage, a hanging water bottle, a package of mega-nutritious rabbit pellets, a zippered bag of rodent snacks, and the world's smallest bag of wood shavings. And so it was I spent just shy of a hundred dollars to turn a wild creature into a pet.

I set him in his new cage on our screened-in porch where he could hear the birds chirping and watch the early morning coyotes roam the banks of the pond. I found him a tiny cardboard box he could duck into whenever he felt insecure. At the weekly cage cleanings, "Peter"—named in homage to Beatrix Potter—would hop into his cardboard box, after which I'd close the flaps, and transport him out of the cage.

As the weeks went by, Pete outgrew his security box but I could still corner him and force him to hold still while I petted him. While I did this, he often pressed his face against the bars of the cage and squeezed his little eyes shut as if in deep and fervent prayer.

The field guide began to nag and admonish:

> *Wild rabbits should be released as soon as they measure five inches in length. The longer you keep them, the more difficult to handle they will become and the less likely their chances for survival in the wild.*

One day, after Pete's lithe and sinewy body had evaded me for nearly a half hour—all that good nutrition having created an über rabbit—I did some soul searching.

"Kid," I told the quivering rabbit, "You are a wild thing, meant to run free and forage for yourself. In my anxiety over your safety, I'm keeping you from fulfilling that destiny."

I set his cage down outside and stood facing the dense, brushy hills that border the property and smelling the verdant breath of spring. Then I opened the cage door.

He seemed to know this was his chance and he took it. The music didn't swell, and he didn't stop to look back at me like in a Disney film. Instead, he focused on the world ahead and scooted into the bushes. My last view of Pete mirrored my first view—a tiny cotton ball.

Letting the Bunny Go

Now, this could be a simple tale of rabbit and human coming to an understanding, but it's really more of a parable. Because it goes this way sometimes with the children we raise. We think we have a domestic species that readily adapts to close quarters, when what we have really raised is a child of a wilder genus—a *Sylvilagus humanus.*

As parents, we struggle against the separation that we fear— that we know is coming, and that is our wild child's instinctive response to being reined in. We cling to them even as they push back with all the savagery and desperation of, well, a caged animal. That's the nature of free will, isn't it? And at a certain point we have to learn ... to open the cage ... and let the bunny go. •

B.E. Jackson grew up among story tellers—writers, actors, and musicians—and learned early the importance of treating an artistic career like the business that it is. After receiving a degree in Psychology, she pivoted to helping people recover from trauma and addiction through equine-assisted activities at her ranch in rural Arizona. In 2012, she published a how-to/memoir on her life with animals, titled *Herdmates to Heartmates: The Art of Bonding with a New Horse.* She is currently working on two novels.

In Search of Solace

by Claudia Chowaniec

I wake up. Dread pressing heavy on my chest. Breathing shallow. Sharp intake of breath. I remember. Today is October 26th. On this day, ten years ago, three small words shattered our world.

I remember the day. I hear our car pulling into the driveway. It's my husband returning from a follow up with his doctor. I'm chopping vegetables and sliding them into the pot of aromatic broth. The onions are making me cry, as they always do. I wipe away my tears. He opens the back door. I hear his footsteps oddly heavy and slow.

I call out, "Hello my love. I'm making soup. Doesn't it smell good?"

No answer. I run into the hallway. He's standing there, slow tears filling his eyes. I've only ever seen him cry once before. When I'd screamed at him, "I'm leaving right now and I'm never coming back."

"Don't," he'd said. "Please don't. I don't want to lose you, my love."

I reach out to hold him. For a split second I feel a deafening silence. I close my eyes.

"I have cancer," he whispers hoarsely.

I open my eyes. I take him by the hand and lead him upstairs to our bed. We lie down, huddling under the blanket, frightened children in a thunder storm. Our bodies meld, pressing together, two halves of a perfect whole.

"We'll get through this," I say. "We'll find the best doctors. We'll research new treatments. We'll do whatever we have to do to heal you."

"Yes. Yes," he says. "I'm not going to leave you."

After a while, on that day long ago, that day with the same date as today, we got up. We hugged each other. We went on with our lives. We never spoke of the possibility of death.

For three years after the diagnosis, the cancer raged chaotically, spreading through his body. Seeking out his organs, methodi-cally, relentlessly advancing.

Seven years ago, I lost the love of my life.

I discovered many ways to escape the truth, the reality of my unbearable loss, my anger. Why us? I traveled almost constantly. I was never at home. I visited friends I hadn't seen in decades. I did not try to put my life in order. I did not try to separate out what had been his, what was now only mine.

I did not empty his closet, throw out the old clothes, give away the good ones to charity. I did have to return his beautiful cherry red leased car. I wept all the way home after dropping it off at the dealership.

COVID 19 changed all that. I had to face myself, to learn to live with myself, to like being alone with myself.

I wonder sometimes, How did I carry on? And it comes to me this morning as I lie in bed. When we wrote our marriage vows, we scratched out "until death do us part" and replaced it with "for everlasting time." Death would not separate us.

That has helped me get to here. To this day. How am I going to mark it, honor and acknowledge it? Do I tell someone? Find solace in sharing with our daughters, a friend?

I choose to mark it for myself. I write. That is what I can do. Write it down, make it meaningful. I write to honor the memory of the life we had. To mark that moment it ended.

Perhaps I can move forward from here, a milestone on my journey in search of solace.

I'm still in bed, drifting in and out of sleep, wisps of memory, old dreams, flowing through me. I'm sheltering here in my heap of pillows, pulling my comforter tightly around me as I often do on these chilly, late October mornings.

My window is open, and I hear street sounds—kids' excited callouts as friends arrive, happily, noisily out there at the school bus stop on my corner. I get up and open the curtains to watch them chattering and running around until I hear squeaky brakes as the school bus arrives.

An enormous crow lands out of nowhere on the top of the tall spindly fir outside my window. It looks at me calmly, its piercing eyes recognizing my presence. We nod. It caws raucously and flies away.

What message is it delivering?

It's 9:10 a.m., more or less the time those three words were spoken so long ago. My cell phone pings, and I look over. An image of my first grandchild appears on the screen.

Is this the message? Is this the answer? I have made it to here. I am moving toward joy. I am finding solace. •

Claudia Chowaniec is the best-selling author of *Memoir of Mourning*. In 2021, Claudia received a grant from the Canada Council for the Arts to write *Moving Toward Joy: how to survive the death of the love of your life and learn to live again*. Published in journals and online, she writes literary non-fiction and poetry; she is currently querying agents. Claudia lives in Ottawa, Canada. Her recent adventures include travelling to the interior of British Columbia to kayak and to photograph grizzlies on the Chilko River and becoming a first-time grandmother.

Signature, Please
by Annette L. Brown

I t began with his words, "A dumb jock in the English Department. That's new."

What? That's how my new advisor responded to why I was attending college out of state! Scrutinizing his dark eyes, I discovered no signs of jest.

When I think about it now, I wonder, would he have called me a "dumb jock" if I were a male? Unlikely. Female college athletes were still new, Title IX having passed just eight years earlier. This equity act provided females with athletic opportunities traditionally available only to men. My advisor appeared to believe that women belonged in their place. I believed women belonged in their place, too. It was just a different place—the result of being raised by a father who claimed he became a feminist the day of my birth.

Nine hundred miles from home, I had left the Central Valley of California, traveled north up the coast, then east over rolling hills of dry wheat to my new home in the Pacific Northwest. The golden, breeze-bent stalks were different from my valley home, lush with trellised vineyards, sweet potato and corn fields, almond and peach orchards. The unfamiliar landscape soured my stomach, but I chose this. I accepted the volleyball scholarship that covered all my college expenses and led me here as a junior transfer.

My new advisor and I considered one another, a not-so-classic faceoff: a black Stetson perched atop his head to a mahogany ponytail dusting my shoulders; a leather John-Wayne vest hugging his chest to a cotton volleyball t-shirt hanging loosely on mine; a handlebar mustache hovering beneath his sharply angled nose to summer-tanned cheeks freckled like confetti. My academic advisor wore the headdress of power. I wore a scrunchie.

"Dumb jock" froze my words, churned my stomach. *Respond!* I turned away from my advisor toward the artwork hanging on the wall—something peaceful with a meadow and stream, a complete contrast to the tempest twisting my thoughts. I wanted to sound mature. I wanted to protect my dignity. I needed to say something. *Breathe. Think.* I was alone for the first time, and while 20 had felt mature on my birthday, it felt inexperienced and apprehensive just then.

The soft tick of the wall clock nipped at the silence. My heart outpaced its rhythm with something like indignation, approaching anger, shadowed by doubt, fueled by frustration. *Do I just swallow his insult?*

Finally, bullied by my own silence, I retorted: "I rarely refer to myself as a 'jock' and never as 'dumb.'" *Breathe.* "I can read a course catalog. Please sign my class list for the semester, and I will be on my way." Even as the words marched from my lips, I feared they were untrue. Could I read a course catalog? Of course. But well enough to be graduation-ready in two years? I shot a glare at his age-puffy, bloodshot eyes while heat gathered in my throat and rushed uphill to my cheeks.

"And you're sassy, too!" He tipped his head back to punctuate his guffaw.

We appraised each other, divided by the wake of his laughter. I could feel my shoulders beginning to slump. "Signature, please," I managed, my fight exhausted.

Navigating new traditions and different people, including my advisor, had challenged my notion of self until my father's voice found me. It had drifted behind, tucked into the corner of a suitcase as I traveled, discovered as I unpacked those final bits of me. His words shielded me from uncertainty. "You can do anything. All you need is a good plan and hard work." Determined, I combed the course catalog, made lists, and double-checked requirements, managing that document with love-letter reverence.

Each semester, I entered my advisor's office and repeated, "Signature, please." Though we exchanged no conversation, my dislike of him grew when he traded his "dumb jock" attitude for a slow smile, eyebrows raised in approval. His gaze prickled my skin.

As graduation approached, I needed one last signature. I had met the English degree requirements, which my advisor knew since he'd evaluated my transcript prior to my entering. Smug, I waited for him to look up. *Magma cum laude–not bad. Right now, it feels good to be "sassy!"*

He leaned back in his chair, wrapped a curl of his mustache in a forefinger, and trailed his eyes the length of my sundress, eventually lamenting, "Well, I guess I won't have you to bounce around on my knee anymore."

What a piece of work! I shook my head—swallowed words gathering in my throat to spit his direction. Faking a smile, I extended my right forefinger—*tap-tap*, a staccato beat on the dotted line. "Signature, please." •

Annette L. Brown is a mother, wife, mediocre cook but competent baker. She lives on an almond farm in central California where she enjoys time with family and friends. She has recently become serious about refining her craft and feels privileged to enjoy the support of two writing groups: the Taste Life Twice Writers and the Light Makers' Society. Annette is inspired by nature, family, beauty, and humor and has had pieces reflecting those inspirations published in *Cathexis Northwest Press*, PSPP's fall 2022 *Twists and Turns* anthology, *Flash Fiction Magazine* and *Every Day Fiction*.

(This story includes descriptions of sexual assault.)

Handful of Gravel
by Wendy Jett

A handful of gravel. It fits nicely in your pocket. The pocket of your jeans. Your coat pocket. The pocket in the side of your backpack or the front of your purse. That's really all you need. One handful of gravel.

No, my mom did not sit me down when I was 12 and tell me all the details about a handful of gravel. My health teacher did not put it on my second-semester test. It wasn't in the "Being a Girl" column in my favorite magazine. I learned the power of one handful of gravel all on my own. While other 7th graders were shoving handfuls of pot into baggies and folding them neatly under their mattresses, I was storing gravel in my baggies.

Sometimes I forgot to pull the gravel out of my pocket before tossing my jeans in the laundry. My mom always thought it was my little sister's fault for the clinking rattle in the washer. I didn't have the guts to tell her it was me.

It was a Friday night, a mid-summer birthday party, moved to the outdoors, by the parents that were tired of hearing the noise that 25 sugar- and hormone-filled pre-teens make. Once outside, we reverted into childhood. We played kick-the-can, flashlight tag. We even caught a few fireflies. Then someone yelled, "*STRAWBERRY BELLY!*"

I hate that game. It's not a game. It's a call to arms. I did not want to be part of throwing someone to the ground, pulling up their shirt and smacking their belly until it became a "red strawberry."

Within seconds of a name being called, a fury of a couple dozen smacking hands began, wielded by kids all basically celebrating that their name had not been called. A torrent of slapping hands can cause some major welts on the belly and deep wounds to the spirit. The look on their face as they are being smacked shows that it's damaging. Even the eyes of the boys glazed over, just hoping it would end quickly and they would have a chance to get even. I just ran around in a circle praying that my name would not be called. "*Strawberry Belly.*" *Who the hell thought of that game?*

Then I heard my name. I took off running as fast I could. I had a slight chance to get away, or maybe delay the inevitable. I felt someone grab my legs. Down I went, face-first into the dirt. Before I could breathe, they flipped me over, pulling my shirt above my head, exposing my new JCPenney bra to dozens of eyes. A barrage of slapping hands began pelting my stomach, stinging, burning, humiliating pain.

"Get her! Harder! Make it red! Burn her belly!" I could hear them shouting. My friends. *My friends*, smacking my stomach and holding my arms over my head. Then someone shouted, "*STRAWBERRY BELLY, … RACHAEL*" and they were off, running frantically after Rachael, their new victim. Everyone, except him.

He pulled up my bra and grabbed my breasts, laughing, and squeezing as hard as he could. I froze. I couldn't move. His knee pushed into my hip to keep me pinned down. His forearm was across my throat. I felt a drop of his spit hit my face. Then his menacing hands began probing, exploring. He unbuttoned my pants, his hand digging between my legs. I yelled. But everyone else was off smacking the life out of Rachael.

Then I saw it. A penis. A real penis. I had never seen one before. It was protruding through his unzipped pants. A poisonous snake searching for prey. I was going to be bitten.

Then I felt the gravel under my head, pushing into the back of my skull. I reached back, grabbed a handful of gravel. One handful. And with it, I found a primal scream that started at my feet. I pushed all that fear and anger into my arm and threw that handful of gravel right into his face. Hard. It hit my target—his eyes, his nose, his spit-covered lips all pelted with gravel.

"You bitch!"

It was the first time I was ever called *bitch*.

I sat up. He stood up. He zipped up and ran after our friends. *Our friends.* I put a handful of gravel in my pocket just in case my name was called again.

Did I tell anyone? Of course not. It was a birthday party, after all. *His* birthday. I did not want to be known as *that bitch who spoiled the party.*

A handful of gravel. I never leave home without it. Because you never know when your name is going to be called. •

Wendy Jett is a born-and-raised Kentucky girl who now calls Lexington home. Mom to two humans and two canines, she does the best she can every day. Some days she does better than others.

A Voice Lost ... and Found

by Richard L. Davis

I did not think I would find them.

I knew she wrote stories—short plots filled with adventure and compelling characters rendered with a graceful, eloquent pen. I read many and enjoyed each. She loved the craft. And loved life.

But did she write *her* story?

I knew I would lose her soon. Too young, she learned to live with chronic headaches and to function despite the pain. She traveled the world—Europe, Japan, Africa; a swim competition off Saipan; whitewater rafting on the Indus and Ganges Rivers. Lots of girlfriends. Furtive attempts at boyfriends.

Then headaches became migraines, then a swelling behind each eye. Surgery, chemotherapy, radiation. Then blessed remission and a return to college, a master's degree, jobs, and over a decade of normality and hope.

But the *Presence* was not done with her. A second recurrence, then a third. More surgery and treatments. The *Presence* proved relentless, and then she was gone. I thought her voice silenced forever, yet I somehow could not believe it. Somewhere I knew she had told her story, but where?

Obsessed with finding her words and once more hearing her voice, I searched her apartment for private notes, letters, and journals. Perhaps a secret diary? I rummaged through closets, the kitchen, boxes in the laundry, suitcases, under mattresses, and her soon-to-be-sold furniture.

A neighbor offered me a good price for the furnishings. Before releasing them, though, I searched once more through the empty drawers and spaces to assure myself I had not missed anything. My hands touched every surface, mindlessly, without direction, feeling their history, remembering the loss more so than the purpose.

Then, as if her words were reaching out to me, I found it— a small journal—previously unseen in the back of a dresser drawer. I held my breath as I pulled it out. The diary dated from her early years, half a lifetime ago, before the *Presence*. Softbound and tattered, its dry, aging pages chronicled the days when her energy, optimism, and hope had yet to be tempered by disease.

Could there be more? Encouraged, I reached in again. Nothing. Then, at the back of the drawer, a small wooden lever beckoned. I pressed it, and a panel dropped, revealing a hidden space. A rich reservoir of memory emerged—five more journals, two autobiographies, steno pads, a dozen notebooks.

Once compiled, the cache covered her entire life from her earliest memories. I held her soon to be reawakened voice in my hands the way I wished I could once more hold her in my arms.

My hands shook and the pages blurred. Wiping my eyes, I read through each precious jewel, often fumbling as I turned a page. She had bought this furniture with its elaborate secret hiding place as a hallowed sanctuary for herself alone. Now, here I stood, treasure in hand, feeling like a terrible intruder. But, read I must.

She wrote of childhood memories in California and Guam, of friends, of writing for her high school newspaper, and of boys. "I felt so comfortable while we danced," she wrote of a young Marine she met in Africa, "almost as if I was 'whole' for the first time in my life. When we parted, I felt like I had lost something (and) I longed for him to hold me again." (31 July 1991)

When the *Presence* took hold (1996), she remained hopeful, giving: "Determination. Love and support. Prayer. They are vital in all aspects of survival," she wrote. Yet, "a part of me feels ashamed. Ashamed that I have years, months, weeks, … more than so many. I want to repay their lives by giving mine to others like them, by becoming that loving, supporting person they may or may not have." (1998)

Migraines continued: "I'm tired of sitting alone in a dark room. I've opened the windows to let in the light and am heading for the door." And yet: "Life's not worth living

A Voice Lost … and Found

without the pain, because we won't learn anything unless we experience it all. ... It's (something) not to fear but to embrace. Because we are not fully alive until we do." (2010)

She concluded: "[We] have a choice every day regarding the attitude we will embrace. ... We cannot change the inevitable. The only thing we can do is play the instrument we have. [The] only disability is a bad attitude." (2012)

On March 13, 2020, her oncologist told her treatment had failed; the *Presence* would continue to grow regardless of what they did. She anticipated what he would say and surprised us. "Part of me is angry," she said. "Part of me is scared, but most of me is just tired." Then she released herself to the inevitable she could not change.

On November 23, 2021, after 25 years of their journey together, the *Presence* took her. She was 48 years old.

Diane was my daughter. Too soon gone, but she left her voice for me to find. My daughter. Diane. •

Copyright 2023, Richard L. Davis

Richard L. Davis lives in Augusta, Georgia, and studied for several years with Amherst Writers & Artists. A retired Air Force officer with an extensive writing history, he has authored multiple professional works but most recently published a novella and has two more manuscripts pending. Currently he is editing and compiling his daughter's journals, which chronicle her decades-long experience with the *Presence*.

Gold Star Mothers

by Thomas Gery

y wife and I were on holiday, staying for a few days at a country B&B. Preoccupied with opening the antique front door lock, I did not notice a symbol of wartime sacrifice on the wall. The circa 1840's red brick farmhouse included fireplaces in every room, wide plank floors, high ceilings and a memorial. A son of America had lived within these old walls. In his place hung an award no one wants—the Gold Star Service Flag.

An antique display cabinet held the memories. A photograph of a handsome youth in uniform hung in the center, the Tropical Lightning patch of the 25th Infantry Division on his sleeve. A group picture of smiling young men in battledress radiated a gung-ho message. GI's mugged for the camera while sitting on top of a $5 million Stryker fighting vehicle. To the right hung the coveted Combat Infantryman Badge earned by grunts who fought in active ground combat. There was a Bronze Star awarded for heroism, a Purple Heart, and, finally, a Veteran's Burial Flag.

I stood there with watery eyes and a thickening throat. My war was more than a half century old, but the display had called up a painful memory. Years before, in 1969, I had refused to talk to a different Gold Star Mother. I was 21, recently returned from Vietnam, separation papers in hand. Once again a civilian, I had thought the horrors of war were behind me.

This other Gold Star Mother's son had been an Army helicopter pilot. When his aircraft was hit by several rounds, he crashed in flames. I was part of the team that went in to pick him up. He was on fire, badly injured. Fourteen days later, the unit's command conducted a memorial service. When the dead pilot's parents learned of my part in the rescue, they wrote to me. I was shocked to learn that they lived 30 miles away.

These parents were reaching out to someone who had been with their son at the end. They assumed we were buddies. They expressed gratitude and grief. They wanted to meet me to say it in person and hear about their boy.

They did not have the full picture. I was not their son's friend, nor did I like him. I saw him shoot at innocent civilians, like a little boy with a BB gun shooting birds for fun. He disdained anyone not white. I wanted no part of meeting his relatives. What could I say? They were desperate to fill in some blanks for themselves and his wife and baby. He was their hero. They were clinging to memory as well as the posthumous medals, and to them I was part of their story. But I had cared little for their memories or their grief and ignored their second letter. Was the solace I failed to give then regret felt now? In this home of an American son did I feel his mother's sorrow or my own self-pity?

Our mornings at the B&B included a full country-style breakfast. As we were our hostess's only guests, she had some time to talk. I drank coffee and listened while she cooked and spoke about her only son, killed by a sniper's bullet in the summer of 2005. She drew a vivid picture of his life before the Army. He had been a good kid, a proficient student, and part of his tightly knit rural community. They were a Christian family involved with their church. Military service was part of her family history. She showed us photographs of men in Class A uniforms with ribbons and medals. They had been his role models. As a little guy he had a GI Joe action figure with uniform and toy gun. He had enlisted after graduation. His parents had hoped he would not, but they respected his decision.

She said the military funeral at Arlington had given her some comfort. As a Gold Star Mother, she had felt honored. Old Guard service members had been present. There had been a casket team, a firing party, a bugler. The grieving woman appreciated the customs and traditions guiding the process of a nation saying goodbye to her boy: the flag draped across the casket later given to her, taps played, three volleys fired, three spent shell casings, three words—duty, honor, country.

The sixteenth anniversary of her soldier-son's death was approaching. So was the fourteenth anniversary of the death of her husband, who was unable to survive the loss of his namesake. She grieved for two. More than fifty years later, I consoled a Gold Star Mother. •

Gold Star Mothers

Thomas Gery, a common man with uncommon life experiences, lives in Berks County, Pennsylvania. He served in the US Army with duty in Vietnam. As a social worker he helped children, youth, and adults in a variety of practice venues and situations throughout a work life of 40 years. Married, with two adult children and two grandchildren, he is currently writing his life story to provide answers to questions his kids will never ask.

The Drive

by Lucinda Trew

When you're commuting to chemo appointments, it truly is about the journey, not the destination.

We've taken this trip countless times, my mother and I. The 35-minute drive is easy on the eyes, and good for the soul—crooked country roads, pastures and farmland, fine stately homes atop sloping hills, and squatty, run-down bungalows. No traffic to speak of unless you get behind a moseying tractor or pickup.

We have watched the seasons change as we've made these drives. From her diagnosis in the spring when the trees were budding—fields freshly plowed, a glaze of pollen on the windshield—to the rich umbers and russets of autumn. We've kept track of the time by noting the progression of sweet corn, from frail bright shoots to tasseled stalks to brittle husks that rasp in the wind.

And though we have seen it so many times, we cannot help but sigh every time when we round the corner where a fine white-columned home sits up high, its filigreed porch spread across green lawn like a lace-trimmed napkin.

On Monday mornings we see gauzy party tents surrounding the Henry Hall Wilson House, where weekend weddings have taken place. We imagine beautiful brides, tipsy toasts, and dancing beneath twinkling lights and lanterns.

She asks me to slow down every time we approach the time and temperature sign at the bank. Time has less relevance now, but weather is something we are mindful of. My iPhone can give me on-the-go updates, but we creep slowly by and wait for the LED scroll to let us know if we should have brought sweaters.

And once we pass the bank, we enter the sleepy town of Monroe, where time seems to have stood still. *Standing still* is a welcome respite, something we would like to hold on to ourselves—an old-school barber shop with striped poles, a service station where they pump your gas and check your oil, an independent video store that somehow survives in the era of Netflix.

The pace picks up a bit when we reach the hospital—not by much, but a bit. We've become experts at navigating the complex of buildings, easing her out of the car, checking in. The expansive drawls of the nurses here match the languor of our drive. 'Sweetie, honey, bless your heart.' Southern terms of endearment that in years past might have grated on my mother's upstate-New York sensibilities now soothe out the wrinkles of why we are here.

As much as we are lulled by the leisurely pace of the town and our bucolic drive, inertia is not an option. We know we have to keep moving forward. And so, she endures the long, indolent drips of chemo—varying rounds and concoctions. She is radiated by a team of kind souls and brings them all gifts of chocolate and thank you notes when she finishes. She listens attentively to good news and bad, does exactly as she's told, is stronger and more resilient than the situation warrants.

And so, we continue making the drive. We take it slower than we did when we began months ago. The jostle of train tracks and potholes are painful to her now. The news we hear takes longer to process. We want to savor the scenery, the day, the time we have.

There are pumpkins now. And sassy yellow mums. Bales of hay and alfalfa bound up in the fields. A chill in the air. Dark that descends earlier, lingers longer.

It all seems too maudlinly metaphoric. But at the same time, just right. We are marking this seasonal passage with our eyes wide open, drinking in the countryside.

My mother grew up in an era of Sunday drives and picnics under sprawling trees. This type of journey is familiar to her; surreal to me. As I drive, she tells me stories of her childhood, her girlhood, her life as a young Air Force bride. Some I've heard before, others are new. Or perhaps I'm paying closer attention now. These drives—and the wise woman occupying the passenger seat—have taught me that: to be present, to slow down, to enjoy the ride.

The Drive

Our positions have switched. I am behind the wheel now, navigating the curves and crises. For so many years, that was her role. She drove me near and far. And she taught me—a most reluctant learner—to drive myself and find my way.

Today, as the road in the rearview mirror gains on us, I am grateful for all the road trips we have shared. We have gotten lost plenty—in conversation, in city traffic, and in places we probably shouldn't have been. I have learned from her that circuitous routes lead to the best adventures. And we always, without fail, find our way home.

And so, we drive, passing produce stands and country churches—and time. We are going somewhere neither of us wants to go. But we are together. On a lovely, meandering road. And for that, I am thankful. •

Lucinda Trew is a poet and essayist whose work has been featured in *Timberline Review*, *Broad River Review*, *storySouth*, *Eastern Iowa Review*, *Mockingheart Review*, *Flying South* and other journals and anthologies. She was named a North Carolina Poetry Society poet laureate award finalist in 2021 and 2022, is a "Best of the Net" nominee, a 2021 Randall Jarrell Poetry Competition finalist, and a *Finishing Line Press* New Women's Voices chapbook finalist. She teaches at Wingate University and lives and writes in Union County, North Carolina.

Oh, Brother

by Stephanie Dean

I f my parents were alive today—they would be proud
of the man who caused them to lose their lives—their
son. He did not kill them—as in murder. Nevertheless,
they lost their health and spirit—then they died.

When my brother, Robert, was born, his plump, rose-colored
cheeks made you want to take your fingers and pinch them.
He was handsome and commanded attention, with his
mahogany brown hair and saucer-like baby blue eyes like
Mamma's. My little brother was the only boy—the youngest
of three. When born, he rocked Mamma and Daddy's world
and because of it, was a tad spoiled.

Mamma's sister, Aunt Sargie, assigned Robert the nickname
"Mr. Tongue" because he talked back so much. Sarge, named
after her army sergeant's way of supervising eight rambunc-
tious younger sisters, saw the handwriting on the wall.
Discipline was lost on the boy. Down the road, lives would be
lost, and someone would pay the price.

When Robert was in elementary school, his quest was money.
I remember Mamma yelling, "Robert, did you take money out

Oh, Brother

of my purse again?" A repetitious exercise of accusations and denials followed. So, Mamma concluded she spent those dollar bills down at the grocery store.

Our neighbor, Dr. Ennis, discovered his gas cans were empty. Robert had enjoyed riding that minibike Santa had left under the tree at Christmas. Dr. Ennis also noticed that behind his home, the woods were missing their usual pop of winter's greenery. Robert had sawed down all the small conifers for a roadside tree stand. A strand of colored lights twinkled at dusk, enticing folks to stop and buy. My brother was not just (only) handsome, he was enterprising.

Robert graduated from a private Christian high school with honors. While in college, he acquired new knowledge. The first year, he lost his new Pontiac Trans Am—it went missing and was never found. So, Daddy bought him a new Trans Am. As bad luck would have it, Robert reported the new car had been stolen. So, Daddy sent him back to college driving his old Ford pickup truck. Unbelievably, the truck was lost, too— stolen—and never found. Authorities never found out the truth behind what really happened.

After graduating from college with a business degree, Robert went to work for Daddy. He became manager, taking the store to new economic heights. Robert enjoyed new homes, cars, boats, and expensive hobby racing cars.

That is, until the day the Snapper lawnmower folks came to count inventory. Just a tiny nudge of a box, and they found out—all riding lawnmowers were missing. Snapper did not find any record of payment, either. The FBI stepped in, and more fraud was uncovered. Because of it, Daddy lost his store and was forced to file bankruptcy.

The newspaper was so insensitive to the family that it featured a lengthy front-page article that read, "Son bilks family out of millions…." After that, the church ladies began showing up at home, bearing gifts—casseroles.

Robert landed in prison. His sentence was one for the entire family, bringing shame and embarrassment. Collateral damage. Our family had enjoyed an upper-middle-class status, living in Nashville's upper-crust neighborhood and attending private schools and exclusive camps. We were called out as uppity Christians by those living below our means. Those whose lifestyle was above ours snubbed their noses and whispered. We might as well have resided on the east side of the Cumberland River where hoodlums lived. People went missing over there—lost and never found. Fortunately, places change, and so do people.

Robert was released from prison. But one prison term was not sufficient to teach him a lesson. Trouble reared its ugly head again—with a vengeance. A life of crime finally caught up with him.

Among the frauds, Robert had forged our parents' signatures on a 30-year mortgage. Title insurance helped to salvage our home, where Mamma and Daddy lived until they died.

Oh, Brother

Redemption came but at a cost. In the end, my brother found his path, released from dreadful compulsions that prompted deceit. Multiple felony convictions and the death of our parents had diminishing effects.

Today Robert is a different person and has found peace. He has grown into the man he was meant to be. Now married, his wife, children, and extended family have forgiven him. He is an adored grandpa to several grandchildren. My brother gained respect from his community and received acceptance and redemption through church.

Amid the crises, I once asked my cousin if I should continue a relationship with my brother. He asked, "If you were lost, blind, and couldn't see, would you want someone to walk with you?"

Over time, I found in our family the calm and peacefulness we had lost in that storm. And the brother I had once lost, I found. •

Stephanie Dean has been sharing her passion for cooking with readers of local newspapers for several years. She has written more than 60 spirited food articles for her food column, "Bless Your Spoon." Happily settled on a horse farm in Mocksville, North Carolina, Stephanie enjoys simple country living. On any given day, one might find her brushing oil across a canvas or hear her plucking the strings of a fiddle. Stephanie believes that whether creating music or good food or dabbling in vibrant paints and flavorful cake icings, the meditative practices are to be savored.

The Lost Spaceship
by Donald Cartwright

I remember being 7 and having dinner with my family at a fancy seafood restaurant. Well, I thought it was fancy because they had real waitresses and those crumbly mints at the register. Best of all were the vending machines in the entrance where you could get oversized gumballs and cheap plastic toys.

I passed right by the stickers and rock-hard gum and went straight for the cheap toys inside clear plastic balls. The quarter went in, the heavy knob clunked over, and out it came.

I'll never forget opening it—tiny, no bigger than the palm of my hand, shiny all over—the most amazing spaceship I'd ever seen, complete with laser guns on the wingtips. Of all the toys ever sold in any of those vending machines, it was the most perfect.

That little spaceship sparked my imagination and became the central focus of my young life. I played with it all day. I drew pictures of it shooting alien bad guys into violent balls of fire. I knew then, as sure as I lived and breathed, that one day I would pilot a spaceship just like it of my very own.

The Lost Spaceship

For the record, I have never piloted a spaceship of my very own.

How long I had it, I couldn't say—a week, a year? In the imperfect attic of childhood memories, it seemed like forever, until, that is, the day it went missing. I don't know what happened to it. Perhaps my mother swept it up along with any number of other small do-dads scattered about my room. The details of my search aren't important, other than to say, it was exhaustive and heartbreaking.

At some point I gave up the search for my spaceship but remained determined to pilot one just like it. I knew astronauts had to fly jets before they could pilot rockets so that's what I would do. I bought a book about fighter jets at the bookfair, and I read it cover to cover. I discovered which jet I was destined to pilot: the Lockheed Martin F-104 Starfighter. It didn't go to space, but it looked like it could, and that was close enough.

Then one day men who smelled like alcohol and cigarettes came to replace the carpet in our trailer, and I overheard one mention the Air Force. That opened the floodgates. I asked him about the F-104, the Starfighter. Had he seen one? Had he flown one?

"Oh, those? Yeah, they don't fly those anymore. They crashed a lot."

So... no F-104 Starfighter in my future. *Fine.* I had plenty of other jets to choose from.

In the 6th grade I learned another harsh truth. Turns out the Air Force won't let you be a pilot if you wear glasses. My father told me this the day I got my first pair, as though that revelation would motivate me to make my eyes suddenly heal themselves.

Fine. That's fine. I was undaunted. Who says I had to be the pilot? I could be a science officer, like Spock. By the 8th grade, I was the school science nerd. My jean jacket was covered in NASA patches, my walls were covered in posters of space shuttles. I had memorized every mission. I had watched *The Right Stuff* endlessly. Nothing was going to stop me from going to space.

For the record, I have never been to space.

It's one thing to be a science nerd, and another thing to study physics in college—takes a lot of complex math, you see. I eventually limped across the finish line to graduate with a liberal arts degree, all the while watching the physics students become physicists, and the Air Force ROTC students become Air Force pilots. Liberal arts degrees should come with free membership in the Future IT Help Desk Workers of America Club.

Fast forward a few decades and it's hard to see the stars anymore with all the light pollution. I still look at the few still visible with the same sense of awe I had as a child, and though I don't know their names anymore, I stop and gawk at every jet that flies overhead.

The Lost Spaceship

I have been blessed in my life and have much for which to be thankful, but some days, when an entire week goes by and I can't remember one day from the next, when I know I will remain unremembered in the annals of history, I think about my spaceship. Did some other boy find it? Is it buried deep in a landfill?

If a boy's love of something could imbue it with a soul, then surely my little spaceship had one. I like to think that if we're not to be reunited in this life and have adventures among the stars, then maybe in the next. •

Donald Cartwright was born and raised in South Carolina. He moved a little over 10 years ago with his wife and two children to Illinois to further his career in IT management. Don has become a respected leader in his company, known for his ability to manage complex projects and to bring out the best in his team. In his free time, Donald enjoys spending time with his family and creative writing.

It's Not the Pearls

by Emily Rosen

It was some time around our 10th anniversary in the early 1960s. He wanted to buy something special for me, and I had a yen for pearls.

We traipsed into "The City" to the jeweler's exchange on 47th Street and exited with a fine choice of long oyster-gems. He peeled off about $2,000 in pocket cash, and we dropped off a dime at the toll booth on the West Side Drive, arriving home, both satisfied with the purchase.

Country-Club, "Stepford Wife," the condition to which I was on the "cusp of," encouraged the sporting of my bauble appropriately at dinner dances and assorted cliché-d gatherings of young matrons, and their fabled spouses of ever-seeking "means." The pearls completed the set of the required acquisitions of the times, which included: the mink coat, the reasonably well-sized diamond ring, and the Cadillac.

And then!

One day, several months later, I could not find the pearls. I remembered having worn them recently. *Had I misplaced them?*

It's Not the Pearls

The silent search was on—drawers, closets, pockets, purses. *Nada!* Days passed, but laden as we were, I had enough trinkets to festoon my body without the pearls, and their lack of presence was not a cause for any great concern—and not yet noticed by my spouse.

Nevertheless, I missed them. And so, to assuage my angst, I stopped at the local Macy's costume jewelry counter and paid $17 for an identical-looking set of long pearls, which elegantly served the purpose on all occasions for which they were in service. And "mum's the word" regarding the switch.

Weeks, months, even years passed, and I happily appeared in long flowing pearls—Macy's best! It went with the total look and no one—least of all my spouse—made any reference to it, except to admire the "total look."

And then!

One day, as I was digging deeply into a drawer in need of a squished item, *Voila!* Suddenly my memory crawled back into my consciousness—including the fact of my having placed the original pearls cautiously into that place. And all the flimsy reasoning behind that act returned to me.

So, now I had two sets of long, flowing pearls. And *dang!* For the life of me, without a magnifying glass, I was hard pressed to distinguish one from the other. Subsequently, I would wear one or the other set—randomly chosen—with a new appreciation for the value of *fake* jewels.

But this is not the end of the story.

As I meandered through the life I was leading, "fakeness" was its ever-present hallmark. We had become part of the fabric of "club life," hedonism its unacknowledged underpinnings. We had frequent "*la-dee-dah*" club meals around circled tables of ten and twelve people. To me, they seemed mostly interested in which restaurants we frequented, where we had traveled, what college campuses we had lounged at for four years, and how "bad" the club food had become.

But business was good, and neighbors became customers, clients, or patients to each other. We were so safe behind the gates. And along our streets, the people had voted to install identical looking green mailboxes, forcing owners to trash the kooky ones, the ugly ones, and the unique ones which dared to mark the inhabitants as possibly people of individuality.

And all this time, my real pearls and my fake pearls mingled together in a jewelry box almost as one, subject to my indiscriminate choice, since I was too lazy to seek the magnifier that would differentiate them.

But time wore me down, and I began to apply a magnifier to the life I was living. Much of what I saw in that glass was a bunch of distortions and a set of values that were misaligned with my own. Slowly and deliberately, I found a life outside the gates. I sought interests and people less attuned to acquisition, those more grounded in trying to solve the aches of society.

It's Not the Pearls

It is many, many years later now. I have had a good, productive life. I don't give much of a damn about the pearls anymore, either set of them. As a matter of fact, I believe I gave them both away during the second major downsizing of my living quarters.

Although I had lost them—and then found them—I had eventually also lost that other me. And with great gratitude, I believe I have found myself again, the *real* me. •

Emily Rosen lives in Boca Raton, Florida, where for over 20 years and until her recent 95th birthday, she instructed classes in memoir writing, publishing two anthologies of stories from her classes, and the book, Who Am I? For two decades and until the local weekly newspaper folded in 2021, she wrote the column "Everything's Coming Up Rosen." Her travel and feature articles have appeared nationwide while her poetry languishes in the pages of a fat notebook. She has worked as a copy writer, travel writer, columnist, elementary and community college teacher, mental health counselor, and owner of the now defunct "singing telegram" company, Witty Ditty. Her long-lived history puts her at an old Philco Radio listening to FDR's "Fireside Chats." (www.emilyrosen424.com)

In the Heart of Trauma
by Arlene Mandell

In 2016, a shocking spate of unprovoked workplace violence throughout the country, and reported on the nightly news, triggered flashbacks of a violent assault with a knife I had experienced when I was 25 and a budding artist. The fear of being attacked again—which I thought I had put to rest—resurfaced and spilled into every facet of my life. Dreading to wake up daily in an escalating state of alarm, I was desperate to escape from myself. But how?

I found a way through "dissociation," a psychological defense mechanism in which you protectively disconnect from yourself. You may not be aware of it, like the woman portrayed by Joanne Woodward in the movie, *The Three Faces of Eve*. Or you may be fully aware, as I was, and disengage from yourself deliberately. This became my strategy—and my problem.

I chose people with the comforting voice I could not give myself, and I took on their persona by mimicking their mannerisms. Though it was all a facade, it felt safer to me to feel like someone else. First thing in the morning, I chose which person to be that day; no one could tell but me. This continued until my brain filled with so many pretend selves,

I lost my real self in the crowd. Confused and overwhelmed, I needed, and sought out, professional counseling.

I responded quickly to the therapy process; telling my story to someone skilled at listening was a huge relief. Trauma can be isolating; those affected tend to keep it to themselves. The therapist told me that often in cases of trauma, the sense of self explodes into pieces and has to be rebuilt. "Let's picture a lean-to," she said, "not super-secure, but enough to keep out the wind." Bit by bit, we would build on that structure till it was solid, strong, and permanent, a structure that would protect me from being blown apart again.

As trust between us strengthened, we began a type of therapy used with anxiety disorders called EMDR, an acronym for "Eye Movement Desensitization and Reprocessing." EMDR uses a patient's rapid eye movements to tone down the intense effect of past traumas. She explained, "We cannot erase bad memories--they are part of us, but we can learn to manage them by weakening their power to control us." Think of telling your story with the ending you really want it to have.

The therapist engaged me in recalling the disturbing event— my being attacked—through a special technique as she checked on my discomfort. By application of this technique over time, we hoped to tamp down and reshape the traumatic incident as I experienced it. With each set of interactions, my extreme fear would become less distressing and gradually transition into positive thoughts, such as: *I did the best I could in that situation.*

During all this time, I was attending a memoir-writing group. Writing *is* therapy, right? Through that group, I learned about the Personal Story Publishing Project and submitted my true-life story of helping developmentally challenged young adults swim with dolphins. How thrilling to see that story published in 2019, then hear it read on the "6-minute Stories" podcast! Personal stories continued to flow through me and compelled me to express them. On National Post Traumatic Stress Disorder Day in June, I wrote down in detail the story of my being attacked, my blood-curdling encounter, the story I had buried for decades. Nervous, I sent the story to several caring friends. I also offered it to "6-minute Stories" podcast.

They said it was an important story and they would like to share it on the podcast if I were interested. Yes! In my late 70s then, I wanted to tell that story. I needed to tell that story. I told my therapist I had made the decision to go public, and although I was afraid, I was determined to go through with it. She offered, "Be afraid, but do it anyway." And I did. My story, "Artist Borne," the story which had controlled me for decades was released on November 17, 2019. I had pushed through fear to tell my artist-story—the cornerstone of my life! Writing my story and sharing my story had changed my life for the better.

In our final counseling session, I thanked the therapist whole-heartedly for her support and for helping me find what was lost. She wisely replied: "Finding yourself is actually returning to yourself. You were there all the time."

Trauma no longer defines me, nor do I need to become someone else. I am one person now. Through sharing my story, I have found my voice; I have come home.

And it's true, I was there all along—but now no longer trapped in the heart of trauma. •

Arlene Mandell lives in Linville, North Carolina, and is proud to celebrate her tenth year as an artist at the distinguished Carlton Gallery in Banner Elk. A native New Yorker and Head Start teacher, relocating with Captain Dan to the Blue Ridge Mountains ignited a love of writing. Her "6-minute Stories" podcasts include: "Eye of the Dolphin," "Artist Borne," "Gobsmacked in the Gulfstream," "Renegade Daughter," "It Started with a Typo," "Shopping for the Homeless," "Thirteen Candles in the Dark," "The Promise of Romance," and "At 5 and 95, Mother Was a Star."

The Worst Day of My Life
by John S. Viccellio

I hated 4th grade in Chatham Elementary. My teacher was impatient, always angry, and mean. I knew she hated us, and I lived in mortal fear of her. Of all the things said to me by teachers in all the years of my education, I can quote one thing she said with absolute confidence: "I'm gonna smack yo'r jaws." It was a clear reflection of her attitude toward me and my fellow classmates.

One winter morning, I had to go to the bathroom. I was afraid of raising my hand to ask permission to go, so I decided to wait the 30-odd minutes until morning recess. Twenty minutes till recess, I was hurting. Ten minutes, I was in agony. Five minutes, I could hold it no longer, and I lost it. I wet my corduroy knickers. I was 9 years old, and I had wet my pants in school. I was mortified. When the bell rang for recess, I was paralyzed with embarrassment, and I stayed in my seat. Somebody asked me why I wasn't going out to play, and I mumbled something about not feeling well.

Class started again, and I was sure everyone was staring at me. My kidneys jumped into double overdrive and kept filling my bladder to overflowing again. I could not raise my hand to get permission to go to the bathroom, because everyone would see my wet corduroy knickers. I was caught between the need to go and my unwillingness to embarrass myself before my classmates. I could not hold it, and I relieved myself again. I sat rigid in my chair, looking straight ahead, making eye contact with no one, holding back tears with every power within me. Every muscle in my body was rigid, except, of course, the ones controlling my bladder.

At lunch time, I did not move. I was locked in my seat. Again, after lunch, my kidneys went back into overdrive, and I kept going. I relieved myself. I went. I did number one. I whizzed. I peed. I pee-peed. I weed. I wee-weed. I tinkled. My corduroy knickers were saturated. My chair filled up and overflowed. It ran down my leg and drenched my knee-high stockings. It ran over the edge of my chair and began to drip. Each drip sounded louder and louder to me, like pebbles falling on a tin roof. The drips turned into a puddle under my chair. The puddle turned into a lake. A tiny rivulet left the lake, became a stream, and then a river flowing over the uneven floor to the edge of the classroom. I looked straight ahead, stone-faced. The class was unusually silent, I thought—none of the normal whispers, talking, or activity.

I was locked in shame. I was bright crimson, not mere scarlet, with embarrassment. I learned forever the meaning of the words "shame," "embarrassment," and "mortification," experiencing each in double measure. I was afraid I was going to die. I was afraid I was *not* going to die. Fear gripped me. *Oh, my God, she's going to make me go to the board and do arithmetic. She's going to make me stand and read aloud in front of the class. Oh, God, please, no fire drill.* At afternoon recess, the class rushed out and avoided looking at me. One of the girls in class came over to me, put her hand on my shoulder, and said, "Are you okay?" I will never forget her simple act of kindness and genuine concern.

When school let out, I waited until everyone else left. Then I ran from the room, ran out of school, and ran home, my corduroy knickers swish-swishing all the way. The cold got to the moisture in my pants, and I felt like I was freezing. When I got home, with tears streaming down my face, I told my grandmother what had happened. She helped me off with my clothes, heated a kettle, and made me a warm bath.

The next day, I had to go to school. No excuse would have worked. As I walked to school, I anticipated the giggles, the whispers, the taunts. I could imagine the groups pointing at me and laughing. But I found that day to be an experience of unsurpassed grace. Not one of my classmates said or did anything to call attention to my disaster, not that day or ever. Everything that day was normal, and they treated me as if nothing had happened. Buddy Haymes still came over to play catch. Cary James still invited me to his house to work on model airplanes, and Ann Whitehead still tried to kiss me after Sunday School.

My 4th grade teacher had not known what to do or what to say, so she did nothing. A few months later she sent me off, jaws un-smacked, to the 5th grade and to a dear, sweet teacher who loved me. •

John S. Viccellio published *Guess What's in My Garden!* in 2014 and *Bacon Grease & Baseball* in 2018. He wrote a monthly garden column for ten years, was a contributing writer for *Carolina Gardener Magazine*. He is a Master Gardener. His blog, *A Walk in the Garden*, has reached readers in over 140 countries and can be seen at johnsviccellio.com. He served 24 years in the U. S. Navy and worked as a computer systems project manager in industry. He lives in Matthews, North Carolina and is a member of the Charlotte Writers Club.

Black Dome Reprise

by Kenneth Chamlee

"We don't maintain that trail anymore," the ranger said, handing the topo map back to me. "There hasn't been a crew down there in a couple of years." Our disappointment must have shown because he added, "It's too far down the mountain, too steep and badly overgrown."

My brother and I were in the office at Mount Mitchell State Park in July 1969, asking about Mitchell Falls, a remote site on the western slope of the highest peak in eastern America. The ranger's answer explained why we had not found any trailhead. His caution, though, was a siren call, an unintended challenge to two former Boy Scouts. Thanking the ranger, we returned to our car, map in hand. We looked at each other and agreed, "We are definitely doing that hike."

We had visited Mount Mitchell before to hike or tent-camp, and we had walked the short path from the parking lot to the summit. At the base of the stone-and-concrete observation tower was a simple grave surrounded by iron fencing, the final resting place of Dr. Elisha Mitchell, the professor who measured the Black Mountains in the mid-1800s and determined they were the highest in the Appalachians. The story's tragic ending is well-known. Mitchell's scientific rival, Thomas Clingman, thought the Great Smokies were higher, and to solidify his findings, Dr. Mitchell, one evening in June 1857, was ascending rugged Black Dome, as the mountain was called then. He fell over a waterfall and drowned.

Despite the ranger's warning, this familiar story pulled us toward the woods. Pocketing the topo map and following the ranger's reluctant tip on where to start, we hiked into the balsam-fir forest that always smelled like Christmas to me. If we had taken time to count the compressed contour lines, we would have seen that Mitchell Falls was over 2,000 feet lower than the summit and not a great distance away across the quadrant. That meant "steep down and steep back." Soon enough, the sketchy trail became little more than ferns and evergreen shoots. We continued, partly guessing our way through the close canopy of laurel and rhododendron which offered shade but no relief from mid-summer heat and humidity. With soaked shirts, melted candy, and nearly empty canteens, we were bug magnets in fading light.

During one of our increasingly frequent rests, we surveyed the surrounding forest, unable to see more than a few yards. If we had been on a remnant trail earlier, clearly, we no longer were. We were not ones to quit a hike, but the approaching darkness and our lack of confident direction forced the issue.

"No way we can retrace how we got here," my brother said.

"Agreed."

We looked at each other and nodded. We knew the road through the state park ran along the western side of Mount Mitchell as it angled toward the summit. If we headed constantly uphill, we would eventually cross the road and could walk to the campground. Going straight up would also be the shortest way, but definitely not the easiest.

Our flashlights did not last long in our upward toil over roots, sharp rocks, deadfall and slippery moss. I tried to put surprised snakes and night-roaming spiders out of my head. Gravity was our guide as we could see nothing in the tangle of limbs and leaves so dense it blocked moonlight—wicked snarls that old mountaineers called "heath-hells." We were not hiking but pulling and crawling as the terrain was too steep and the headroom too low.

For several hours we dragged and kneed and elbowed our way uphill, until at last we heard the whoosh of a car and saw a streak of headlights through the trees. In a few minutes we collapsed on cool grass beside the pavement, thanking the stars that were then visible. It was not our finest hour as young explorers, but we had not panicked once certain we were lost. We had survived—scratched up and exhausted, yes—but unhurt and relieved no rescue party was involved.

The next summer, spurred by a gnawing sense of failure and stubborn determination, we undertook the Mitchell Falls trail again, this time starting much earlier in the day, packing more water and snacks, and now a bit wiser thanks to remembered wrong turns and better map study. We found the falls and the quiet pool where Dr. Mitchell died. As we munched our apples and peanuts in that gloomy spot, I imagined it looked much the same as it had 112 years earlier, when a resolute geologist-minister ventured there with the certainty of his conviction and a single fact to prove. Sadly, he lost his life, but Elisha Mitchell's name is forever fixed to the woods and the wind of the tallest mountain east of the Mississippi River. •

Kenneth Chamlee's work has appeared in four previous Personal Story Publishing Project collections, and his poems have been in *The North Carolina Literary Review*, *Tar River Poetry*, *Cold Mountain Review*, *Pinesong*, *Kakalak*, and in many other places. He is a 2022 Gilbert-Chappell Distinguished Poet for the North Carolina Poetry Society and teaches regularly for the Great Smokies Writing Program of UNC-Asheville. A book of poems, *If Not These Things*, was released from Kelsay Books in 2022. Learn more at www.kennethchamlee.com and @kenchamlee on Twitter.

To the Tall and Caring Man
by Lisa Williams Kline

When my daughter Caitlin was about 4, I lost her at a craft festival. I had our younger daughter, Kelsey, in the stroller, and Caitlin by the hand, and we were at an old fairgrounds in Rockville, Maryland, on a crisp blustery fall day, weaving from booth to booth with wood carvings, watercolors, silver jewelry, and dreamcatchers. The crowds were prodigious; I chastised myself for even being there and trying to navigate the hordes of people with the stroller, but I was hoping to find unique Hanukkah and Christmas gifts.

Caitlin came into the world wanting to be in charge. I must admit, even as a toddler, she wrested control of many a situation from her mild-mannered Southern mom.

I can't exactly remember why I let go of Caitlin's hand. The stroller may have gotten caught on the edge of a display and I needed two hands to dislodge it. I may have had to blow my nose. Maybe I even took a few seconds to admire and touch one of the things on display, and truly, I have felt guilty about that possibility for decades. Motherhood, with children that age, can turn on a few seconds of inattention.

The next moment, Caitlin was gone.

I did not panic at first, because it had literally been only a few seconds, and how far could she have gone? I wheeled the stroller around a nearby circular rack with colorful knitted sweaters and shawls, thinking she might be hiding among them, which she had done before. When I didn't see her bouncing blonde curls and blue jacket there, I ran back to the booth we'd just passed, and looked for her. Not there. And then back out to the walkway fronting the booths, teeming with people. Not there, either.

It had literally only been one or two minutes. My heart was pounding, blood was roaring in my head, and I started to call "Caitlin!" at the top of my voice. People turned to look. A panic greater than any I'd ever experienced gripped me. Had someone snatched her? Had she just wandered away? Was she lost and terrified, looking for me? A wave of nausea warned me that my life as I had known it might never be the same. By this time, Kelsey was crying, because, even as a baby, she had sensed something was terribly wrong.

Then I saw a very tall man walking slowly through the crowd, carrying a toddler with curly blonde hair and a blue jacket high on his shoulders.

I screamed, nearly collapsing with relief, and then raced to get to her, angling with the stroller through the people, probably knocking down a few.

"Oh my God, Caitlin, oh my God!"

LOST & FOUND

The tall man leaned down and delivered her into my arms.

I clasped her to me so tight. I was crying with relief, Caitlin burst into tears, and Kelsey, who had already been crying, continued to wail.

Before I could gather my wits and thank him, that tall, kind man faded into the crowd.

Maybe it wasn't exactly on that day, but after that, I decided I would never—at least figuratively—let go of her hand again. Because Caitlin always wanted to go her own way, our relationship was volatile at times when she was an adolescent, but I did not let go. Those were some tough years, and we tried a lot of strategies, and probably made a lot of mistakes, but still, I did not let go. And eventually, grace and time brought her back to us.

Years later, our family has drawn closer, and Caitlin, now in her 30s, is literally the glue that holds our family together. Of course, she still insists on being in charge. She is the one who plans the menus for Thanksgiving and Hanukkah and Christmas and Passover. She is the one who organizes surprise birthday parties and trips and shows up to help unpack when one of us moves. She would never abandon any of us. Recently, her sister Kelsey had a dangerous health situation. When she heard, Caitlin said, without hesitation, "If she has to have chemo and loses her hair, I'll cut off mine and give it to her. If she can't have children, I'll be a surrogate for her. She's my sister." It did not happen because it did not need to happen, thank God, but Caitlin was sincere.

To the Tall and Caring Man

I have wished for many years to be able to offer adequate thanks to the tall and caring man who carried her on his shoulders back to me. To us.

So, thank you, sir, from a grateful mother's heart. •

Lisa Williams Kline is the author of two novels for adults forthcoming in 2023, *Between the Sky and the Sea*, and *Ladies' Day*, as well as an essay collection titled *The Ruby Mirror* and a short story collection titled *Take Me*. Her stories and essays have appeared in *Literary Mama, Skirt, Sasee, Carolina Woman, moonShine review, The Press 53 Awards Anthology, Sand Hills Literary Magazine*, and *Idol Talk*, among others. She lives in Davidson, North Carolina, with her veterinarian husband, a cat who can open doors, and a sweet chihuahua who has played Bruiser Woods in *Legally Blonde: The Musical*.

Deathbed Promise

by Linda Vigen Phillips

I adored him. I inherited his Nordic features, his love of poetry, his vast curiosity, and his adventurous spirit. He spoiled me rotten as his only child, and forever prized me as "his punkin." He said, use your own good judgment, long before I earned it. He was 44 and barely home from WWII when I was born.

He never went to college. In fact, whether he graduated from high school is questionable, but he was whip smart. He enlisted right before marrying my mother and ended up in the 99th Bomber Group in Italy. That may have been his undoing, detonating those bombs. At his age, enlisting had been entirely optional. I asked him once why he did it. He told me there was something pulling him in. He could not explain it. My mother loved him enough to wait it out for three years.

My mother lost her innocence as a teenager to a wayward guest at the hotel her parents owned in eastern Oregon. My grandfather must have blamed her because he sent her away to nursing school in Portland. Within days she was picked up by the police without money or clothes, muttering incoherently about seeing angels and being tested by God. After this psychotic break and a 3-month hospitalization, she met and married an alcoholic with whom she had my sister, Patty. That marriage dissolved quickly, and the two of them moved to southern Oregon where, on the eve of WWII, she met my father.

I have few memories of my early childhood. Maybe that's a good thing. A mentally unbalanced mother, a probable PTSD father, a rebellious teenager, and a spoiled toddler stuffed into a tiny one-bedroom bungalow set up slim odds for avoiding a train wreck of a family. After a too-long stay in a crib, I graduated to a shared bed with Patty in a make-shift bedroom on the made-over back porch. Depending on her mood, Patty called me a whiny brat, cursed me with foul language she learned from my father, shoved me against the wall in bed, or avoided me altogether. The memories of my mother during those early years are like the shadowy background of a dark painting. She was present but largely disconnected. I would later learn how she struggled to function on the heavy medications she took to ward off manic episodes.

Some good memories remain. My father built every model in the Tinker Toy brochure while I handed him the pieces like a surgical nurse passing the scalpel to the doctor. He was the one who read books to me every night. In winter, he pulled me in a red wagon through a foot of snow to the neighborhood grocery store. In summer we gathered driftwood along the beach to make a fire, roasting hot dogs until the Pacific Ocean was put to bed by an orange sun. Often, my mother sat alone in the car.

My sister, during an occasional truce, allowed me to watch her build a model home for a school project—three bedrooms, two baths, a garage and a fenced-in yard. I was fascinated by the three tiny matchbox beds with colorful bedspreads, each enclosed in a room with a door that locked. We shared an unspoken bond that day in our separate imaginations, but I would never guess the deep significance this exercise had for her, far beyond a school project—bedrooms with doors that locked.

On her deathbed, my sister made her husband promise to tell me what she never could. The same year of the model house—I was 5, she 15—my father sexually assaulted her in that bed we shared. Maybe being shoved up against that wall spared me, because I have no recollection of the incident. But the blurry memory of the moments afterwards have haunted me all my life: me, cowering in a corner of the kitchen while the three of them shouted and screamed obscenities, my sister wielding something in her hand. It was a knife, my brother-in-law told me. Patty put a stop to him that night with the threat of a kitchen knife.

My brother-in-law delivered this news to me shortly before he died. No family is left with whom I can fact-check the story, but I know these things to be true. My father loved me and guided me through difficult years with a mother with bipolar disorder. For this I am eternally grateful. The fact that he was a flawed man who tragically lost track of his own good judgment does not nullify what he did for me. I have found peace in forgiveness. I cannot change what he did to my sister, or its devastating effect on her. I continue to hope that she has found that room of her own where locked doors are no longer necessary. •

Linda Vigen Phillips' poems, essays, and flash fiction have appeared in such places as *The Texas Review*, *The California Quarterly*, *NC Poetry Society Award-Winning Poems*, *Wellspring*, *Windhover*, *The Friends Journal*, *Moonshine Review* and more. She has two published YA novels in verse, *Crazy* and *Behind These Hands*. She recently studied with poets Dannye Romine Powell and Jessica Jacobs to complete her first chapbook, *For Survivors to Consider*. She lives in Charlotte, North Caroliina, where she is a member of Charlotte Lit and Charlotte Writers Club.

One Soul Alone

by Janet K. Baxter

D uring a recent visit, Linh was again agitated. He spoke rapidly and jumped topics frequently.

"Mama, I cry sometimes. I can't stop." Linh gripped my hand hard with his cool, thin fingers. I look up into his dilated eyes, wide with terror and sadness. I grip his hand back tightly.

"Business is OK, Mom and Dad," he then declared. "New managers…" The litany of thoughts spilled out rapidly one after another.

"It was bad when we were in China, Mama." Linh's focus shifted to the past when he was 11 years old. "It was bad for Hang. Being a woman. It was bad for women." This was the first time I'd heard this story about his sister. As a youth, he had talked of the small boat crashing off the China coast, swimming to the beach, hiding in the woods by day, walking up the coast at night. The small band of refugees dug small shellfish on the beach and boiled them for soup. It took months to reach the refugee camp in Hong Kong. His recollection was usually reticent and restrained, not ever sharing specifics. He never told us what he experienced which torments his memories.

When Linh joined our family, he laid out clean clothes each night in preparation for school the next day. He learned English quickly and made friends. He earned his black belt in Karate and played high school soccer. Linh earned an art award his senior year; one of his paintings hung on the back wall of our church for years. We did not know that he lay in his bed most nights trembling with fear.

After high school, Linh's life unraveled before our eyes. He had five traffic accidents in one year and part-time jobs that he lost one by one. In college, he partied and drank heavily. Linh also proudly became a naturalized U. S. Citizen.

Over time, Linh's problems were increasingly serious and complicated. In his mid-20s, he agreed to speak with a therapist, but I could never convince him to return. Instead, Linh ran from his demons, speeding to outrun the nightmares of his escape from Vietnam and the experiences that altered his young life forever.

At first, he told us he left our area for summer work. However, Linh eventually moved permanently to New York City. Because Linh spoke English, he found work within the Vietnamese community interpreting for English-speaking customers for the non-English speaking staff. Linh immersed himself in the Vietnamese culture. At the time, his spoken Vietnamese was immature and child-like resulting in ridicule among his Vietnamese peers. So, he spent time with

Vietnamese families to become fluent with the language and culture. His cultural identity was shaken. Was he Vietnamese? Was he American? He did not fit anywhere.

The defenses Linh had developed as an adolescent did not support him in adulthood. He avoided his emotions and memories. He was the "big spender," the big man at the party. His car was repossessed and he repeatedly accumulated large debts. When he visited, we noticed that he had lost weight and rarely made eye-contact. Conversations were filled with information to remove our worries, yet he evaded questions about his welfare. He "faked good" with his stories, talking rapidly and forcefully, allowing little opportunity to question or dig deeper. At meals, he ate ravenously and took leftovers to eat afterwards.

Many years later, I had a moment to connect with Linh. He was thin and exhausted, sad and emotionally fragile. His litany of personal problems spilled out during our conversation.

I put my hand on his arm that was shaking under his dark, long-sleeved shirt in the summer heat, and asked him one question, "How long, Linh, are you going to be unhappy?"

Linh looked up at me, his eyes finally meeting mine.

I repeated, "How long are you going to be unhappy?"

We talked at length, finally connecting in a conversation that was uncomfortable for Linh. Linh moved back to our area the following year. He has become a licensed nail technician; his

One Soul Alone

natural artistic talent is shown in his nail designs. He quit smoking, after having smoked since he was 7. He has a dog. He guzzles energy drinks for breakfast. Linh is adamant he does not take drugs, but his dilated eyes and rapid talk tell on him. His PTSD symptoms continue to haunt him. Now in his early 50's, Linh has lived independently for almost 30 years. Yet, he attends and enjoys all family holiday get-togethers.

Linh calls weekly just to see how I'm doing. "I'm OK, Mom," he says over and over. "Don't worry about me."

But I do. •

Janet K. Baxter lives in Kings Mountain, North Carolina, and is a member of the Charlotte Writer's Club and Scribblers, a memoir critique group. Her stories, "Horse Whispering for the Average Woman," "Southern Blues," "A Frank Lesson," "Cappie, The Boomerang Horse," "An Angel's Smile" and "Morgan: Our Escape Artist" have appeared in previous anthologies published by the Personal Story Publishing Project. Retired, Janet enjoys her new passion, thread painting, as well as dabbling in writing, trail riding, and keeping up with all the critters on her 'mini-estate:' www.mountaingaitacres.com.

Taking Flight

by Akira Odani

My 19-year-old son Minoru vanished. *He could be dead, lying sick, who knows where, or a fugitive running from the law.*

In the winter months of 1989, he disappeared from the campus of the Florida Institute of Technology. He wanted to learn to fly airplanes but not by attending college classes. He dropped out of school and was evicted from the dormitory.

Years of my wrangling with my wife and his parents' inevitable bitter divorce in New York had contributed to his alienation. He had been slipping from my grasp throughout high school. The freedom of campus life must have been disorienting to a young man who had lived under the intense supervision of his mother, a Japanese who respected strict discipline.

How frightened and lonely he must have felt! Weeks went by without a whisper. I imagined the worst. To help launch a rescue and recovery mission, I recruited his younger brother, Shigeru, still in junior high school, as my emotional crutch. Our first stop, the college housing office, offered no information. We searched for one of Minoru's friends, who told us he had seen

Taking Flight

my son at a poolside party some days before. *He is alive.*

"Have you seen an Asian boy, tanned, with dark hair, five foot nine?" After two days of tracking fragments of information, an address emerged as the potential location. Through the dirty, frosty glass of the bare window of an isolated, abandoned-looking apartment building, we peeked and found him sleeping on a bare mattress on the cold linoleum floor. We knocked hard on the plywood door. "Minoru!"

"How did you find …?" he started to ask as he emerged, scratching his oily, bushy hair and rubbing sleepy eyes.

"With difficulty," I declared.

We uttered a joint sigh of relief and celebrated our reunion with the one diet Coke he had in his fridge. Minoru agreed to return home to New York.

After that setback, he found a job on the ground at the White Plains Airport. The film *Top Gun* and Tom Cruise had tickled his imagination several years before. He donned a padded flyer jacket on ski slopes and to school, even on warmer days. Dozens of model airplanes with insignia, decals, and coloring filled a display cabinet—fighter jets, antique aircraft, and passenger airliners, including a DC-10, L-1011, and Boeing 747.

Months later while I traveled to Tokyo for business, my ex-wife reported Minoru joined the United States Navy. I winced that he had not consulted me, but I appreciated that he took the initiative to advance his career. But I regretted that we never discussed "war and peace," especially the horrific history in the Asia-Pacific War my Japanese family experienced a generation ago. I prayed he would not be killed nor kill anyone.

Did he find his new life secure within the discipline of the military organization? After more than a year of silence, I resigned myself to the cold reality—my son did not want to reach me. The guilt of believing I was a failed father grew heavier. The hollow space in my heart filled with a dull ache.

One morning in late spring 1991, however, I received a phone call from him.

"Son! How are you?" I suppressed my quickened heartbeat and tried to sound casual.

"Good, Dad. Listen. I'm graduating from a flying school in Tennessee. There'll be a ceremony this Saturday. Would you like to come?"

Not only was the call unusual, but his invitation was unexpected. *He wants me to be with him!* I danced within and booked the flight immediately.

When I arrived at the designated hall of the Naval Air Technical Training Center in a suburb of Memphis, I found Minoru chatting with his classmates, all wearing uniforms: the Army, the Navy, the Air Force, and the Marines. My son, with a golden tan and a gleaming smile, wore the crisp white attire of a sailor with a blue neckerchief.

Taking Flight

The presiding officer took the podium. He congratulated the class and presented a certificate to each student. In alphabetical order, the young men and women stepped forward and received their diplomas with a salute. When my son's name should have come, it did not. Fumbling with the program, I reexamined it. Minoru's name was listed separately at the bottom.

"Now, ladies and gentlemen, for our top graduate, United States Navy Machinist's Mate Airman Minoru Odani."

The pronouncement boomed like a cannon, rendering me deaf for seconds. As I swallowed the news, I stood and craned my neck behind the crowd to capture the moment on my camera. The presiding officer motioned me to come forward to gain a better angle. Blurry. *Was it the lens or my eyes?*

My son beamed like a soaring hawk with his prey in his beak. I recovered my once-almost-lost son and embraced him on that day when he found his own wings. •

Akira Odani lives in the ancient city of St. Augustine, Florida. He is a member of the Taste Life Twice Writers' group and the Florida Writers Association. Born in Tokyo, he wrote extensively in the past for the Japanese media. Still, more recently, his interest has turned to writing in English and on subjects related to his memories of interacting with the two cultures. Some of his work has appeared in the pages of FWA anthologies and PSPP's fall 2022 collection. He stays active, meditating, swimming, and playing pickleball.

The Gift

by Cherie Cox

Still coming through the haze of Christmas-week surgery, I recognized this as January, another year. And I was still alive.

I had shown up for my writers' group at a local coffee shop, six weeks post-operative. One critic found my last chapter, "choppy, unlike your usual, authentic voice."

True, through the fog of dopey, double mastectomies in 13-hour surgery, I might have lost the zing and fervor for my coming-of-age novel. My passion for the 1920's and a young woman's conflicts, had awaited my survival. Unsure I could return to a half-finished story, I wrote anyway. The latest feedback felled my confidence. My writer's voice stopped, caught in crossfire.

Up to that point I had faced mortality and won. My 30-year profession as an assistant public defender had its blessings and challenges. I had retired in time to write my novel. It was half-finished when I faced the cancer battle. It had been growing quietly, undetected by annual exams and mammograms.

I received the call-to-surgery for Christmas week. Perhaps a wiser woman had cancelled, leaving a vacancy in a season no one wanted casualties or disasters. Fearful of waiting, I entered, coming out breastless and confused.

I felt alone, despite a week in hospital, with young nurses, wearing antlers, helping me to eat food and to get to the bathroom. A day before discharge, a cheery young aide announced, "Time to get out of bed and walk." She opened a basement window to December sunshine. These working soldiers tried. But my self-image had become less real; I was the walking wounded.

Weeks later, I sought consolation among fellow writers. After an hour in "critique hell," I was wandering across a parking lot, heading to the nearest grocery store, determined to stock up on comfort food, even knowing I could barely eat.

Inside, I stood for minutes in the pet food aisle, labeled "small animal needs." I had those, but it took a while to find the ice cream and the coffee.

Basket full, I soldiered on to the check-out. A brightly scarfed cashier offered her open aisle. She reminded me of the hospital aide, that certain smile. Unloading all my angst on that conveyer belt, I barely heard her voice.

"Miss D.A., how have you been?"

Looking up I saw a woman greeting me, dark curls peeping from beneath her scarf. I did not bother to correct the misnomer.

"I am doing okay," I said, struggling with small courtesies. "And how have you been?" I said, faking it.

"You don't remember me," she said, relieving me from the truth of nonrecognition.

She lifted a bag of cat food from my cart and continued talking as she rang up the cookies,
ice cream, frozen dinners, and other odd items I did not want or need.

"I was so rude to you when we first met," she added. "I am sorry."

I was still trying to recall her. Maybe she knew me from the courthouse.

"Oh, but, by your smile, I take it we came out okay, then?"

"You won my case!" she said. "You changed my life."

"I did that?" I asked.

Faint memory was returning. I remembered a seriously bitter woman, dressed combatively in camouflage, and heavy boots. She had been unhappily accused of assaulting another woman in a fight over a boyfriend. She could barely manage a civil word, at that time. Her bright demeanor and dress were not the same today.

"Oh, you told me if I went to court with a scowl on my face, the judge would certainly see only that scowl. And you made me even angrier when you asked if I might consider dressing less combatively. I said I had a right to dress the way I wanted. I was so insulted." She paused, shook her head. "But my brother told me you were the best lawyer up there and that I had better listen to you. Glad I took that advice."

The Gift

79

The conveyor belt paused.

"You taught me how to be a lady!"

I smiled, the first real one I had managed in an eternity of six weeks and many trials. In her presence, I was finding my voice again.

"Oh, I am certain you were always a lady. How good to see you happy! I am sure that all we did was polish up a bit, together."

"Do you mind if I come around and hug you?"

"Well, of course not," I allowed. "You cannot imagine how much you have helped me today."

She came around the counter, and I reached out, accepting the gentle hug. We finished checkout.

I have greeted her, and she has greeted me several times at that store. I suppose we lift each other's spirits. Cancer has not come back. And even though my writers' group has since dissolved, my authentic voice has returned. •

Copyright 2023, Cherie Cox

A published news journalist and a practiced lawyer, Cherie Cox calls North Carolina home. Awards include the Charlotte Writers' Club first place in poetry. Published short stories, essays, professional legal articles and poetry vary her credentials. These include *Personal Story Publishing Project* anthologies, *Kakalak*, and *The Christmas Wreath*. She enjoys people who give their best effort. *The Hickory Daily Record* and the Mecklenburg County Public Defender's Office enriched her life. Many individuals inspire her respect of the written word.

Pop the Kettle On
by Rose-Mary Harrington

In 1958 in England, I was 7 years old, and I was allowed to make tea as I was able to reach the gas burner on the hob. My mother and her best friend, Daisy, would supervise, seated at the wooden kitchen table that stood under a generous picture window looking out to the garden. I would gingerly open the tea caddy and spoon loose tea, one teaspoon for each person, into the teapot. After I poured the boiling water into the Brown Betty, I would cover the pot with a hand-knitted tea cozy, which would keep the beverage hot. I retrieved the tea strainer from a drawer and held the strainer over each cup to catch the leaves. I delicately poured the tea into floral cups with matching rose saucers on which rested teaspoons to stir the beverage. My preference was tea with two sugars and milk. My mother liked lashes of milk; Daisy had a penchant for strong tea with heaps of sugar.

I was squashed into the corner of the table by the windowsill. I sipped my sweet hot tea and eavesdropped on my mother and Daisy's endless commiserations about their husbands' shortcomings. I received an education in relationships and decided then and there I would never marry, or worse, be beholden to a male of the species. Whenever strife presented itself within family and friends the problem was resolved with a cup of tea.

When Daisy confronted her unfaithful husband, Jack, in our kitchen, between sobs Daisy kept repeating the word, "Philanderer." My mother insisted, "We must all calm down and have a cup of tea." The potion must have worked for Daisy and Jack survived 60 years of sometimes wedded bliss.

We lived in a basement flat which was part of the railway station. Friends would kill time before catching a train up to London and drop by for a cup of tea and conversation with Gwen, my mother. Gwen embraced the chatter and gossip as long as their points of view aligned with hers.

Every Thursday for 40 years my mother served tea to Mr. Seymour. Mr. Seymour worked as an official for the railway and was assigned to take care of my mother after she was widowed. He continued that duty way past his retirement. Mr. Seymour was six foot two inches tall, immaculately attired in a blue pinstripe Saville Row suit, a starched white shirt, conservative blue tie, and shoes that mirrored ceiling lights. His hair was a silver mane and his eyes steely blue. In his youth he had been a ballet dancer, then a fighter with Lawrence of Arabia, riding a camel into battle. He followed this by joining the British Navy during World War I He could not swim, and when his boat was torpedoed, he clung to a rock for 11 hours until he was rescued. My mother and I were a captive audience listening to his stories and adventures. I do believe that Mr. Seymour was secretly enamored of my mother. Gwen was a blousy, blond intellectual who had fallen in social standing due to her second marriage and the war. Gwen had many admirers as she was outspoken, especially her mantra of 'Women can do anything.' During my childhood I concocted never-ending cups of tea for visitors to Stanmore Station. "Pop the kettle on darling," was the resounding request from my mother.

When my mother died in 1993 of a brain tumor in hospital, during visiting hours, the head nurse popped her head through the blue striped cotton privacy curtains surrounding my mother's bed and body. "Let's make you a cup of tea love, in my office." The head nurse made the tea, handed me a chipped cup as my tears diluted the brew.

In 1970 when I immigrated to the United States, I forsook tea. Good black tea was difficult to procure, and I wanted to assimilate into the culture and as it is today, "a cup of Jo" is a mainstay of the American diet. In the late 80's I married an Englishman. We had met in Arizona and we serendipitously both originate from the same village in the home country. Tea became a staple of our daily lives. Every afternoon around four or five o'clock we gather as a family. My youngest daughter, who is decades older than 7 is requested to "pop the kettle on." Either my husband or I will complete the task of making the tea with Yorkshire Gold Tea which now is sold in bags. Our teapot is clad in a quilted tea cozy to keep it warm. I insist my tea is strong with a splash of milk, without sugar. Each family member has a Spode teacup. We assemble in the living room, sip our tea, and talk about our day.

I am grateful I rediscovered my taste for tea. •

Pop the Kettle On

Rose-Mary is originally from England. She now resides in Wilmington, North Carolina. Rose-Mary is on the board of Port City Playwrights. Her background is in theatre. Currently her play *Six Seconds* is in pre-production and will be staged in November 2023. Rose-Mary recently received an Arts Council Grant to produce an audio recording of *Six Seconds* which will be available on YouTube. Rose-Mary is inspired by her five muses and nine grand muses. They all enjoy a cup of British tea in the afternoon.

In Transition

by Jane Satchell McAllister

Having enjoyed near-perfect health my entire life, I find myself surprised and completely unprepared for the changes in my body and health entering my senior years.

What possible evolutionary benefits exist for thinning hair on my scalp and errant chin whiskers on my face? The age spots on my hands resemble a sepia-tone Jackson Pollack. I sometimes wonder whether I am missing much with my reduced hearing capacity. Cataract surgery and vaccine responses figure into conversations with friends. Learning prescription drug names poses as great a challenge as negotiating Russian subway station names in Cyrillic. Please tell me I am not the only one who wanders around the house looking for the eyeglasses perched on top of my head.

The pleasant challenge 20 years ago of practicing yoga poses requiring balance and flexibility now represents a Sisyphean task. Falling Tree pose anyone? Our Pit bull performs the only Downward Facing Dog pose in our house these days. I joined my niece's weekly Zoom class for brisk 30-minute exercise sessions focused on core strength. When did 30 minutes become such an interminable duration?

A fast metabolism since childhood let me eat whatever and whenever I wanted. Now, dinner later than 6:30 guarantees a restless night with a too-full tummy. My usual nightly glass of vino retired along with me; waking up with a fuzzy head got old faster than I did.

Such minor irritations fade in light of more pronounced changes requiring attention. Discovering that I had developed extremely high cholesterol, my physician recommended a statin. My life-long aversion to taking pills led to a year-long struggle over necessity and dosage until one day my best friend wisely advised, "Grow up, it is something outside your control, and I have been taking statins for decades." So, that health challenge is better managed, though I continue to feel piqued with the daily pill taking.

In the process of studying aging, I read a book by a respected physician on the factors that seemingly contribute to longevity and a healthy brain. The book provides a useful checklist of risk factors and action plan for tackling the issues. I am in trouble from the starting block. Not since my first pop quiz in 8th grade Spanish have I scored so badly on an assessment. Clearly, work needs to commence.

Aggravation and humor vie for dominance as new issues crop up, and aggravation usually wins. However, with a life outlook grounded in optimism, I acknowledge that aging has brought many happy changes in retirement, relaxation, and reflection.

I walked away from a fulfilling, stimulating workplace as the director of a small county public library into retirement, grateful that I could do so. I embraced the opportunity to set my own schedule, travel more, read and write more, and invest more time with spouse, pups, and friends.

While travel has consistently been a part of our lives, retirement enables us to travel across our country for much longer periods of time, even to the remote wilds of Big Bend National Park in southwest Texas, where I ascended the steep Lost Mine Trail for splendid early morning views—even though I did not set any land speed record. Adding car camping, backpacking, and kayaking to my repertoire opens up more spectacular wilderness areas.

In retirement, social interactions with friends, neighbors, and community seem easier to arrange. Dinner get-togethers with friends feature enjoyable conversation and much laughter. An informal book club gathers avid readers discovering new authors, some of whom begin to feel like old friends. Several college-era friends stay connected with daily text exchanges of Wordle scores, accentuated by periodic visits and travel. Walking the pups around the neighborhood ensures at least one pleasant conversation with neighbors almost daily.

Perhaps most importantly, time for reflection abounds. I may not have made a splash on the world stage, but hopefully my work with the public library and the local humane society has generated lasting, positive ripples in my local community and among my circle of acquaintances.

In Transition

If the final curtain falls at death, then I wish for a legacy of kindness, accomplishment, and adventure. If reincarnation awaits, then I hope that good karma makes me a volcanologist the next time. If a spiritual afterlife follows my last breath, then I tremble in eager anticipation of reuniting with loved ones including my beloved dogs. Regardless, I feel tremendous gratitude for the life gifted to me and joy for the experiences and people that accompany me along the way.

Now, what new discovery awaits today? •

Jane Satchell McAllister's writings draw inspiration from the wide variety of people and places she encounters, from her home base in Davie County, North Carolina, to rich adventures across our country and abroad. She has co-authored two *Images of America* books through Arcadia Publishing and served for nine years as director of the county public library. Her current writing project is compiling stories based on decades of travel, both fiction and non-fiction, almost as much fun as the trips themselves.

The Application
by Landis Wade

Completing an application is meant to be an exercise toward a more perfect, hopeful, exciting, and fulfilling future. That's the way it was for me when I completed my application for my first driver's license, for the job I held for 35 years, for my license for a marriage that has survived for 39 years, for the loans on my first and second homes, and for the birth certificates for my children who, as adults, have completed their own life-changing applications. In fact, I can't remember a time in my life when completing an application did not give me an anxious but good feeling until recently, when I filled out what they call a "Petition for Transfer to Inactive Status to the Council of the North Carolina State Bar."

My dad was the one who encouraged me to go to law school. A lawyer himself and knowing my uncertainty about what to do with my life, he said, "Landis, you can do anything you want with a law degree." I suppose he was right. I met Janet in law school, who put up with me in marriage, and who gave me two bright and adventurous children.

Mom and Dad attended my law school graduation ceremony. Mom gave me a big hug. Dad shook my hand and gave me one of those smiles that said he was proud of me. The State Bar was all business though. They assigned me lawyer number 11134, a number I've known by heart for most of my life because it was my ticket to practice law, represent clients, earn a living, raise a family, and try to do some good every now and then for those who could not afford to hire a lawyer to help them.

Dad's gone now and I wonder what he would think about my latest application to end what I put so much time and energy into achieving. Honestly, I'm not sure what I think about it myself. The decision to retire was made four years ago, and I have not practiced law since then. So, the decision to give up my law license makes sense. But why am I sad? And why is it that the first thing to pop into my head when I looked at the petition was the excitement I felt at being accepted to law school and meeting my new classmates at orientation?

I wonder if nostalgia is a feeling someone has when the time comes to sign divorce papers? Does the final act—the execution of the right, inevitable decision—bring everything good about the relationship into sharp focus? It feels like I'm losing something important. It's the reason my hand hovered over the signature line for a few seconds. And when I walked my decision to the mailbox, I thought how typical this process is of lawyers and laughed. You have to apply to get into the club. And once you're in, you've got to apply to get out.

I decided to retire from the law because I wanted to do something creative in my 60s. Did you hear the one about the lawyer who walked into a podcast studio? That was me, a bad joke about a guy who gave up good money for no money and who didn't know the difference between a mixing bowl and a mixing board but who thought it would be fun to interview authors and learn more about how to write. Four books and more than 500 author interviews later, I do not regret the decision. My life has been enriched by the writers I've met, the books I've read, and the books and stories I've written with the techniques I stole from the authors I interviewed. And yet, my hand still paused over the signature line.

The Petition for Transfer to Inactive Status is full of legalese and boilerplate, saying, in part, that when my petition is granted, I acknowledge that I can no longer practice law in my home state of North Carolina. I can imagine the State Bar approving the petition at the exact moment the last leaves fall from the trees and the season changes. It will be a cold but clear day, and if I wear the right clothes, it might be invigorating to take a walk in my new shoes.

Completing an application is an exercise toward a more perfect, hopeful, exciting, and fulfilling future. Lawyer 11134 had a good run, but the road is wide open now.

You were right, Dad. You can do anything you want with a law degree. •

Landis Wade writes light-hearted legal thrillers and mysteries with a historical or holiday touch (cozies with a bit of a thrill). He is a recovering trial lawyer and host of *Charlotte Readers Podcast* where he has conducted more than 500 author interviews. His recent novel–*Deadly Declarations*–has won six awards, and counting, including Winner in the 2022 American Fiction Awards in the Cozy Mystery category. His essays have appeared in five earlier anthologies by the Personal Story Publishing Project.

My Father's Photograph
by Bob Amason

This year my dad would have been 100. He died of heart disease 20 years ago. But even in life, his heart was scarred emotionally by the war. Of course, to Dad's generation, there was only one war: World War II. The Second World War undid him emotionally in ways that I can't truly fathom. Believe me, I tried.

My father was a warrior. Dad had two trucks shot from under him at Pearl Harbor. Later, he was a tank commander in the 3rd Armored Division in Normandy. The 3rd Armored suffered tremendous casualties. He saw plenty of death. How he survived is anyone's guess. Divine providence. When he died, I hope he went to Valhalla, the warrior's heaven of ancient Norse myth.

My father was demanding. Though he left the Army in 1946, in many ways he was a product of nine years in uniform. Dad set expectations that no one could meet. He was a natural extrovert—friendly and a born salesman. Dark shadows lurked behind a tough, pragmatic outlook. Caring but open to hurt, he took no prisoners. Dad was restless and always seemed to be in motion as though staying busy would hold at bay whatever demons were gnawing at his bones. Oh, he was plenty sane, just haunted.

Dad had issues with women his entire life. Maybe this was because he was an orphan. He really liked women, but when they were not perfect, he would be disappointed. Then they would fight. Some pop psychologists would tell you he had trust and anger issues. Doesn't take a PhD to see that.

Among the few photos of my father from the war years is a snapshot of him in Hawaii. It is dated December 28, 1941. Hand propped up against an Army truck, omnipresent cigarette casually caught between index and second finger. Thick, well-groomed, wavy hair, his face a drawn, half-smiling, pensive, hard-eyed look at the lens. Three weeks before that photo, men around him died suddenly. Their unexpected deaths from a hail of Japanese gunfire and bombs were shocking to all. Paradise had been lost when the attack on Pearl Harbor snatched a sleepy America into WWII's cauldron of death and destruction.

The hard face in that 1941 photo was merely a younger version of the man I knew. Only when the situation demanded would he try to put on a big smile, but I knew that smile was not quite genuine. He was often blunt, occasionally mean, frequently petulant, sometimes generous, and always sensitive. Mostly he was just pissed off. My mom and I knew WWII had changed him. Just how much I did not know until just recently.

Two weeks ago, a family member sent me a formal portrait of Dad taken in December 1939 in his Army uniform. He had just secured his first promotion, and his brand-new private first-class stripe was proudly displayed. My Dad's strong handwriting was inscribed on the back of the photo with a gentle message of love to his aunt. He was just 17. The photograph is still as crisp as the day it was taken. His eyes are bright, his smile huge. Happy face, no lines, thick, wavy hair, optimism of youth. At 17, the world is his oyster, and he is a genuinely happy young man.

Until two weeks ago, I never knew the 1939 photo existed. When I saw it, my heart soared with delight at being introduced to the man who would become my father. In the photo, he is frozen in time. You can see the hope, optimism, and joy of living. His pride at having succeeded in the U.S. Army is unmistakable. After the war, he might have been a chameleon, but in that photo he is real.

That 17-year-old boy was lost to World War II, as were so many others, both the dead and the survivors. On the morning of Dec. 7, 1941, the happy 17-year-old boy in a private's uniform was washed into oblivion and replaced by a tired adult with a hard, troubled look. It was a look that fully overshadowed the million-watt grin of just two years earlier. In one terrible morning full of both fear and courage, my father's youthful outlook was obliterated and replaced with palpable strain and uncertainty. It was the curse of his generation—the *Greatest Generation*.

My Father's Photograph
95

Perhaps he is in a warriors' hall in Valhalla. If so, I hope he sees reflected in the brilliant blade of a Viking sword the happy, hopeful young face that was lost some 80 years ago.

The 17-year-old private first-class was my authentic father. When I saw that youthful face, I said, simply, "Oh."

I had found my father, the hidden man I never truly knew. •

Bob Amason is a retired US Air Force Lieutenant Colonel who was a college professor for 25 years. A member of the Florida Writer's Association, Bob writes under his pen name, Frank A. Mason. Bob's works include historical novels, most recently *Four Women of the Revolution*, and *Blue-Green for the Grave*, a modern suspense novel. His writing has been published in two anthologies as well as academic journals and books. Bob lives in Florida with his overachieving wife, a professor who is author of a series of children's books.

The Sound of Music

by Alexandra Goodwin

It has been six months since I had a total thyroidectomy. The journey toward recovery has been nothing short of bumpy. From the list of possible complications, I had them all. And in the process, I lost my voice, at least as it was prior.

Ironically, I have always been known as the "quiet one." Besides being downright judicious I was also painfully shy. I would sit through social events nodding, smiling, sighing, and listening while others talked themselves to oblivion. Noisy parties shined a light on my husband as he always seemed to have an endless supply of interesting stories to tell. I tagged along, happy to enjoy the limelight from the shadows.

It was not until much later in life that my mother, sensing my desire to be heard, for a change, advised me to imitate him. "Act," she said. "Watch him talk, observe people's reactions, and his reaction to their reactions. And then do the same." I did as she told me. And thus began my gradual immersion into community, kinship, and true connections. Detached from the fear of rejection, I went after that "Oscar" like a root to water, and I learned that people liked what I had to say. By putting on an act, my authentic self emerged like a butterfly from its cocoon.

I embraced the new me. Or was it the real me uncovered? I loved listening to people but also bouncing ideas and exchanging thoughts. My personality blossomed and all those silent years became a thing of the past. A couple of years ago I even found myself on stage, singing karaoke on a cruise ship, for the first time in my life. (Yes, it helps to know that you will never see those people again.) My world was harmonious and full of melody, until I woke up from surgery.

What happened during surgery is known only to the doctors and nurses present at that time. All I know is my last word was "one" as I counted down from three while a resident anesthesiologist covered my mouth with an oxygen mask. When I woke up three hours later, my voice was no longer mine, and months later, I'm still struggling to recover it. Unable to modulate pitch, questions come out as statements, and singing is no longer something I can do. Our home grew silent again as doctors advised me to refrain from talking when their original prescription to talk as much as possible failed to produce the desired results. I explained to friends and family that talking on the phone would be replaced by texting and *WhatsApp*-ing until further notice. I found myself nodding, smiling, sighing, and listening all over again—an unfortunate case of *déjà vu*.

I became increasingly anxious as a deep sense of loss drove me to despair. Mom to the rescue again, she encouraged me to write. So, I wrote. My voice can be heard through the silent lines of ink by those who take the time to read them. Still, I grieve.

Talking to my Rabbi about my predicament, I concluded there is a reason for all this, a hidden message, a lesson to be learned. Knowing why God had allowed this to happen might help me to accept it. *What was the purpose behind losing my voice? What teaching did I need to harness as the days unfolded in the inability to connect to others?* I posed these questions continuously to cope with my unwelcome disability. Struggling to see the light in the darkness and to keep my thoughts positive takes all my energy.

Today, I was driving to visit my mother. The radio was playing mellow rock, but my index finger kept pressing different stations. My attention span has become as frazzled as my nerves. But I wish you could have been there and heard what I heard when I tuned into the mellifluous, raspy, and oh-so-blessed voice of Louis Armstrong as he sang:

I see trees of green
Red roses too
I see them bloom
For me and you
And I think to myself
What a wonderful world.

Wow. There it was. Driving down Holmberg Road, I realized that I had been too busy feeling sorry for myself, which prevented me from noticing how beautiful the world can be.

The source of spiritual strength that had eluded me up until now was right there in front of me—in the trees, in the roses, in the voice of Louis Armstrong. At that moment, I found inner peace. What a wonderful world it is, indeed. •

Alexandra Goodwin is from Buenos Aires, Argentina. She lives under her mango tree where her desk is except when there is a hurricane. She's the author of *Exchange at the Border*, *Whispers of the Soul*, *What Color is Your Haiku?*, and *Caleidoscopio*. Her essays and poems have appeared or are upcoming in *Ariel Chart*, *The Centifictionist*, *Loch Raven Review*, *Stick Figure Poetry Quarterly*, *The Miami Herald*, and *Twists and Turns*. This is her second story for the Personal Story Publishing Project.

Alone in the Woods

by Suzanne Cottrell

Our June Saturday plans change with one phone call from our neighbor Robin.

"A toddler's missing. Can you help?"

My eyes widen and water.

"What's wrong?" asks my husband.

I raise my hand and swallow hard. "No yardwork. A toddler's missing. We've gotta help."

Our daughter asks, "Where?"

"A wooded area near Toler Elementary."

We remove our garden gloves and scramble to the car. When we arrive at the school, the cafeteria buzzes with weary volunteers. We receive our team assignment, sit on plastic seats too low for adult bodies, and wait. As officials review data and point on maps, we lean and listen to their low-pitched voices to glean bits of information.

Last night after dinner, a mother fed their dogs. Her toddler and a dog

Alone in the Woods

wandered into the woods. With her husband, she combed the surrounding area for over an hour before contacting the Granville County Sheriff's Department. Officers searched all night but found no leads.

I bow my head, thankful for a warm summer night.

I wring my hands while questions stream through my mind. *Is he hurt? Where could he be?* I clear my throat. *How could she not notice her son was missing?* My nails dig into my palms as I recall when our 4-year-old daughter Sara played hide and seek in a circular clothes rack. My pulse raced while I shouted her name, darted among racks, and pushed clothes aside. *This can't be happening.* Face flush, my muscles quivered at the thought of a stranger kidnapping her. *Where can she be?* Agonizing minutes later, she popped from behind the blouses. She smiled as I hugged her. "Stay where mommy can see you," I'd admonished. I sigh now, berating myself for accusing a mother of negligence.

A haggard team of volunteers with downcast eyes, wearing sweat-stained T-shirts, shuffles into the cafeteria. They receive water bottles while their leader shares the grim report: *no sighting.* With sagging shoulders and aching backs, we wait, and recheck the wall clock.

With an uncertain tone, Sara asks, "When do we get to look?"

"Soon, I hope," says my husband.

My gaze ping-pongs between the officials and the clock, which reads five o'clock, 23 hours since Connor and his dog disappeared.

My husband says, "Let's go home, get dinner, and come back."

LOST & FOUND

We nod. As we approach the command table, our team's number is called. *Finally.*

After receiving instructions, we cross US Highway 96, fan out, and form a horizontal line. My brow wrinkles, and my eyes dart between Bob and Sara while we plod through the unfamiliar woods. The thick undergrowth of Virginia creeper and Carolina horsenettle grabs our ankles. "Ouch!" Burs stick to our pants. "Hey, watch out. Poison ivy," I say while I swat a spider web. We yell for Connor, hoping he'll scream and reveal his location. We swipe at the brush and scour the ground. Gritting my teeth, *where could he be?* Before traversing a muddy creek bed, I grab my sides and sigh, not prepared for what we could find. We plod through rows of reseeded pines like soldiers readied for deployment. I wipe sweat from my forehead. As twilight limits our visibility, I squint and urge our daughter to stay close.

"Mom, are we going the right way?"

"I hope so."

My husband assures us we'll reach Goshen Road if we walk straight between the columns of trees. When we break through to the road, people on ATVs ask, "Any sign of Connor?" We shake our heads. They wave us to climb on board, and they transport us to the school.

After two hours of trudging through the woods, we drag our sweating, weary bodies into the cafeteria and chug bottles of water. Our leader's voice cracks as he files the report: *no sign.*

At nightfall, the search continues with ATVs. We return home. *Why couldn't we find him?* At a loss for words, we slump on the couch and stare at the television. Twenty-six hours have passed. The odds of finding the toddler diminish.

When the phone rings at 8:30 pm, we cringe, expecting the worst. "Thank you. Wonderful news." My body tingles with warmth. I thrust a fist into the air while the pitch of my voice heightens. "They found him! They found him!"

"Where?" asks my husband.

I gasp at the thought. "A mile from his house, sitting on a stump."

Our daughter tugs my arm. "Is he okay?"

"A few scrapes, thirsty."

We grin, hug, and mumble a *thank you and love you.*

Later, a TV interviewer reports a man on horseback heard a dog bark and discovered Connor and his dog. We were grateful neither was lost and alone, but with each other, just as was our family and our caring community in that time of need. •

Suzanne Cottrell, a member of Taste Life Twice Writers and NC Writers' Network, lives with her husband in Granville County, NC. An outdoor enthusiast and retired teacher, she enjoys reading, writing, knitting, hiking, and Pilates. Her prose has appeared in numerous journals and anthologies, including the Personal Story Publishing Project, Inwood Indiana Press, Quillkeepers Press, and *Parks and Points*. She's the author of three poetry chapbooks: *Gifts of the Seasons, Autumn and Winter* ; *Gifts of the Seasons, Spring and Summer* ; and *Scarred Resilience* and a hybrid book, *Nature Calls Outside My Window, A Collection of Poems and Stories* (Kelsay Books).

The Mezuzah
by Ginny Foard

O n the phone, she said, "The door's locked. Push the buzzer, I'm here."

Late on Friday afternoon, I drove to a Nashville synagogue that I'd found by an online search. I wanted a housewarming present from their gift shop. My friends' father, Arthur, in his late 80s, was living on his own for the first time in over ten years. He and his partner were separating their homes.

The winding driveway led me to the synagogue's parking lot. I parked and walked to the large entry door. I pulled my jacket tighter in the chilly, fall dusk. I was alone.

The door was locked. A ray of light gently glowed far inside the building. *Could that possibly be an open gift shop?*

I pressed the buzzer. The door unlocked. I guessed my way forward to the well-lit gift shop.

"I called about mezuzahs," I said to the lady who let me into the shop.

She smiled, "Here are the ones we have."

"There are so many!" I stepped over to a display shelf.

"Take your time, I'll be in the back. Shabbot services don't start for another couple of hours. It gets busier then."

"I noticed a police car in the parking lot."

"Oh, we always have one here. And the locked door. We're a synagogue," she answered without thought.

The mezuzahs were handmade, containing prayer scrolls. Colors, sizes, and styles dazzled with variety. Some were shiny new, others ancient. Each had loops at the top and bottom, with nails for a door frame.

A brushed gold and bronze mezuzah with metal twisted into a network of flames (or maybe Hebrew script) caught my eye. It was beautiful. Nothing else was similar. The artist was a recent Russian émigré.

"I have a question," I confessed. "I want to give a mezuzah to a friend, but I'm not Jewish. He's in his 80s and is just starting to live by himself. He might need a mezuzah for his door. It would be a housewarming present. Is that okay?" Spoken out loud, my question seemed silly. "Is there any Jewish tradition …"

She nodded, "Well, there's the ceremony to place a mezuzah on the door. A prayer, a gathering, a blessing."

"He'll know about that," I said. "He helped found his synagogue. I just don't know if someone who's not Jewish should give a mezuzah to a Jew. Is that a problem?" I worried about unfamiliar religious customs. Arthur had enough stress in his life, I did not want to add to it.

"I don't see a problem. You can return it, if you need to," she reassured me.

As she rang up my purchase, I noticed a pamphlet describing the synagogue's history. I added it to the bag containing the delicate mezuzah.

I was proud that I'd navigated the mystery of finding a synagogue where I could buy a mezuzah, and that I had found a special one. I couldn't wait to share it. I boxed it up.

I mailed it to Arthur's daughter Terri who lived near him. I didn't have his new address in the Seniors complex. Terri would get the package to him.

"Dad," Terri called across the cocktail lounge, "you've got a package!"

Arthur was having afternoon wine and snacks with his new neighbors. Some were old friends who also attended his synagogue. They'd seen Arthur and his wife Elsye raise their daughters. They'd seen Elsye lose her struggle against breast cancer. She was so young, they all thought. Later, they saw Arthur find companionship with a widowed member of the synagogue. They knew Arthur well.

Arthur smiled. "Here's my daughter. Bearing gifts! … Have a seat, what do you want to drink?"

Terri handed him the package. "Look what came for you." She smiled, enjoying the unknown. Her dad wasn't fully settled in his new home. Gifts were good.

The Mezuzah

Arthur tugged at the wrapping. Out came the mezuzah and my note with the synagogue's history pamphlet. Arthur lifted the mezuzah while holding the pamphlet in his other hand.

"Look!" he whispered. "It's from the synagogue where Elsye and I were married."

Arthur's mezuzah protected his home as he settled in, enjoying family and friends. Eventually, his health declined.

One day, my mail had a package from Arthur's other daughter, Pam. We'd been friends through life's ups and downs. I'd gone to Pam's Bat Mitzvah. Together, we'd helped break our high school debate team's gender barrier. In 1974, I'd caused her not to be with her dad at the baseball game when Hank Aaron broke Babe Ruth's homerun record.

With her package, Pam wrote, "Terri and I wanted you to have a little something from Dad. Thought this was appropriate!"

Months earlier, Arthur had joined his love Elsye in the cemetery.

Pam says she'll help me attach the mezuzah to my doorway. •

Growing up in the South means learning life lessons from family stories. Ginny Foard learned a few things that way. She also found out that later you get to tell stories, too. Depending on who's in the room with you, you might need a few hours to get to the bottom of what all happened. Ginny likes exploring, sharing, and listening to the stories around her. She lives in a little post office box on Sullivans Island, South Carolina.

Finding the Perfect Pumpkin
by Rebecca S. Holder

"Look what I found!"

It was a familiar exclamation from my husband. He has an uncanny ability for finding things, extraordinary things. Walking through parking lots and big-box stores? He finds money, not pennies and dimes, but *folding* money. A hike in the woods? The dropped charm bracelet, an inlaid pocketknife, forgotten binoculars. Even in graduate school when I accompanied him to the library stacks, I heard that excited whisper as he stumbled upon an obscure article or photograph that would become the proverbial cherry atop his research paper.

As he entered our house on this cold, rainy, early November evening and dug deep into the flannel-lined pocket of his field coat, I expected nothing less than someone's bulging wallet, a Rolex watch, or perhaps the Hope Diamond. Instead, he held out an orange tabby kitten, so small it did not fill his palm. The tiny bit of fluff squeaked a faint mew that sent our chihuahuas, Rexx and Prissy, into a frantic, bouncing dance at my husband's feet.

Mark had been working on a vacant unit at our apartment complex and as he parked his truck, he noticed a furry lump in the middle of the street. How awful, he thought, someone's pet was run over. The lump moved. Upon investigation, it was sadder than he had imagined. There lay a mother cat and her litter of six, all dead save the tiny tabby. He scooped the kitten up and took it to the apartment. A couple of French fries from the trash and a container of creamer from his morning coffee order were mixed into a thick slurry for the starving kitten that he now held before me.

Mark carefully set the kitten down in front of the prancing dogs. Rexx took a sniff, determined he wanted nothing to do with it and walked away. Prissy, however, nosed the kitten, picked it up in her mouth and carried it to her bed. The kitten then received the most ferocious licking and cleaning ever given. Prissy had a baby, the kitten had a mother, and we had a new member of the family.

The next day, the vet determined that the kitten could not have been more than five weeks old and would not have survived if my husband hadn't found her. Yes, a "her." There was nothing left to do but assign her birthday as October 1, 1995, name her Pumpkin in honor of the fall season and her color, and schedule the spaying and shots.

Prissy raised Pumpkin as a proper dog. Pumpkin would run to the door with the dogs and try to "bark" at delivery people, a growly meow adding much needed bass to the chihuahua yips. She would sit up and beg for table scraps, had her favorite rawhide chew, and come when you whistled. Though we knew indoor cats had much longer life expectancies, we opted to make Pumpkin an indoor/outdoor cat. She would wander happily outside until we came home in the evening to let her in to dinner and bedtime with Prissy.

We'd had Pumpkin a little over a year when we moved to a new home. We thought our little family was settling in well to the neighborhood even though one neighbor said they despised cats, and another commented about chihuahuas being barking rats. Then Pumpkin disappeared.

For two days, around the clock, we searched for her. One of us outside on the porch always, whistling and calling, whistling and calling. The morning of the third day, I was outside whistling when through the drizzle, out of the woods, came Pumpkin. She could barely walk, her head twisted around at a peculiar angle, blood trickling from ears, eyes, and nose. Panicked, we rushed her to the vet. She had a head injury. Given the nature and location of the trauma, the vet surmised it had been deliberately inflicted by someone.

It was a long recovery, but Pumpkin made it. At the end of the ordeal, the vet said if we ever needed to re-home Pumpkin, he wanted her. Seems she wooed the entire staff because she was a hugger. Whenever they lifted her from her cage, she would wrap her front paws around their necks, pull them towards her and nestle her head under their chins. It was something she had done with us since she was a kitten.

Finding the Perfect Pumpkin

After her injury, Pumpkin's head always had a slight tilt, and her balance was a bit off. But she persisted in being an indoor/outdoor cat, defying the odds when she died from cancer at the age of 13. My husband did not find a wallet, a watch, or the Hope Diamond, but he did find a perfect Pumpkin that November. •

Rebecca S. Holder lives in Winston-Salem, North Carolina and is a member of Winston-Salem Writers. With the advice and guidance of the Westenders critique group, she is working on a short story collection centered on the fictional town of Braidy Creek. When not immersed in fiction, Rebecca indulges in personal essays and poetry. Her story "A Tap at My Door" appeared in the PSPP anthology, *Twists and Turns*. Most recently, she was a finalist for the 2022 James Hurst Prize for Fiction with her story "Virgil Thompson's Salvation".

Six Minutes to You

by David Inserra

W hat was I getting myself into?

It was Friday night, and Route 3 traffic was atrocious. Crashes and breakdowns filled the extra hour I gave myself to travel. When I pulled into the *Sports Pub* it was shortly before 7 o'clock. I had made it just in time. Inside the pub, hip-hop throbbed in my stomach as it echoed over the speakers. Fancy lights flashed about the darkened room and muddled conversations filled the air as drinkers and drunks milled about.

How could they choose a place like this for *Six-Minute Speed Dating*?

Years of being the primary caregiver for my mother had taken a toll on my personal life. So, I was here to do something for me. I was going on a date—many dates, in fact. I would use this time to practice talking to women, work on my social skills, be myself.

I would probably never see any of these women again, I figured, so what did it matter.

A sign directed the speed daters to an elevated room high over the main floor. I choked back the nerves and climbed the stairs to the upper room.

A small group of people, supposedly ages 45 to 59, socialized around the appetizer table. After 15 minutes, the facilitators called for everyone's attention and gave us our instructions. They issued clipboards so we could document "first impressions," "deal breakers," and the like. We were broken into pairs and assigned to one of ten tables or couches. After six minutes, they would ring a bell. The women remain seated. The men move on to the next dater, working their way around the room. After the speed date, all participants were instructed to go online and to vote. If you and the other person each say "yes," your follow-up date would take place in a secure online chatroom. Sounded simple enough.

The bell rang. I was ready. Ten women. Six minutes at a time. Six minutes at one table. Six at the next.

I started at a table with a woman wearing a tuxedo. She never brought up what she was wearing, and I never asked. After asking another woman what she did for fun, she droned on for the next six minutes about her grandson's baseball games and her granddaughter's soccer games. And what about the one with personal space issues? Well, when the music started again downstairs, I slid closer to her so we could hear each other. The woman shrieked and threw herself into the arm of the couch, the only thing keeping her from crashing to the floor. That's the way my night was going.

Then I reached the tenth table—the last table—and Ellen, a blond with sparkling blue eyes. She wore a casual, flattering long, blue dress with a delicate floral print, her smile shining with intoxicating brilliance.

Conversation began. Connections were made.

We were both the same age. Both musicians. Worked as trainers. The list went on. When the bell rang, the speed date was over, and they collected the clipboards. Ellen and I moved to the corner of the upper room and kept talking. I suggested if a question came to mind, we should ask. Ellen agreed. When I wondered if she was in debt, Ellen playfully slapped my arm and said, "I should have asked you that." She had two children from a previous marriage, so I asked if she was divorced or separated.

When they closed the upper room, we went outside and walked around the building. The ease of communication was encouraging. I even told Ellen that I was my mother's primary caregiver, and she did not run away screaming. This woman was exceptional. She listened carefully and fed her curiosity with questions. I asked about her life, passions, hopes, and dreams. Ellen responded from the heart, without hesitation. Two-and-a-half hours later, our *Six-Minute Speed Date* ended. I told Ellen I would love to see her again, but I was leaving the country the next day for work. She laughed, thinking I was joking, … but it was true. Ellen wrote her email address on a piece of paper and slipped it into my hand. "Write me," she said with a smile.

Six Minutes to You

We hugged. We said our goodbyes.

As Ellen drove away, my mind raced with future possibilities.

The house was dark when I got home. As I passed Mom's door, she called to me, asking about my evening. I told her I had met the woman I was going to marry.

I emailed Ellen that night. Again, when I was in Canada. Again, and again.

The facilitators of the *Six-Minute Speed Date* said it was for fun and we should not expect to meet the love of our lives.

They were wrong. •

Copyright 2023, David Inserra

David Inserra and his wife, Ellen Titus, recently celebrated their 13th wedding anniversary. They enjoy life on Hilton Head Island in South Carolina with their dog, Mindy. David's most recent work appears in the PSPP release, *Twists and Turns*. He is a member of the Island Writers Network and works at the local Unitarian Church. David's first novel, a speculative thriller titled "In Your Own Backyard," is currently being queried to agents. He is also a musician who has written over 400 songs, most being about his wife.
Visit davidinserra.weebly.com.

Finding Joy in Borrowed Time

by Patricia Joslin

Where is the mid-size strainer that is always on the second shelf to the left of the stovetop, that is always nested within the large-size strainer? Did I use it to drain the jar of capers or the plant-based noodles I cooked on Thursday? Did I use it to smack the fruit fly that has been making its way around the kitchen counter all week? Is it still in the dishwasher? Hmm. It will turn up when it's not needed.

Fortunately, when I misplace my Google phone I can always ask Alexa to find it for me. I simply talk to Alexa on the Kitchen Echo device. She rings the phone so I can race around the apartment in search of it. If I don't hear the ring, it's either that I have left the phone plugged into the port in my car, or I am losing my hearing too! Though I am not a tech-whiz, I see the value in some of these household gadgets.

But what about the blue stone necklace I want to wear that matches perfectly with the earrings I have in my hand? I want to look cool enough to ice my poetry reading tonight. Is the necklace in the bottom drawer of the chest that holds my mother's costume jewelry or in the plastic shoebox beneath the bed? I search for, then find, tiny pearl earrings that I have not worn in ages, but no necklace. Hmm. I'll put aside the blue stone earrings and instead I'll wear the earrings I just found along with my mother's pearls. Now where did I hide those pearls for safe keeping? And where should I put the blue stones?

The shoes I'll wear tonight are somewhere in the closet - perhaps on the top shelf with the "good shoes" I seldom wear. Or maybe mixed in with the flip-flops I keep on the closet shelf off the laundry room. They could be anywhere or nowhere. Maybe they made their way to Goodwill with the black plastic bag I dropped off last week.

As I think about my misplaced—not "lost"—items, I'm transported back to the 1950s, remembering when I fell in love with the Borrower books by Mary Norton. I was an avid reader who walked a mile or more to the public library every Saturday. Nancy Drew mysteries were my favorites, but I also read Charlotte's Web by E.B. White and the Narnia books by C.S. Lewis. I've forgotten the details. But for some reason the stories of the Borrowers have stuck with me for over 65 years. Those little people were similar to Gulliver's Lilliputians but much more kind and clever.

Perhaps the food strainer, necklace, and mid-heel dress shoes have been "borrowed" by the little people who live in the walls of this apartment. The strainer might have been used to build a cage for a tiny bird that sings. The blue stone necklace would create a lovely focal point for the space just above the fireplace in the Borrower's apartment. And those dress shoes are the perfect size for a child's slide. Oh, such creativity!

Today I placed an order for the five-book boxed set of *The Borrowers*. I'll wrap the gift in birthday paper for my soon-to-be 8-year-old grandson. We'll read the books together and find joy in imagining the small people who take our things and use them in new ways. I'll give my grandson a good comeback line when his father asks him where his shoes are if not in the hall closet. *The Borrowers needed my shoes, Dad!*

As I age, I know that I will lose my energy, perhaps some mobility, and maybe memory. I'm not concerned (just yet) when I misplace my car keys, forget to make an appointment, or call an acquaintance by the wrong name. There is much to lose over time, but so much more to gain when I live in the present moment. I'm slowing down the hours so I can take pleasure in the moments. For now, I have equanimity. I have found peace with this thing called aging.

Author's Note: By the way, the food strainer must have slipped between the shelves of the cabinet, then lodged in a place where only a tiny bit of the handle showed. Was it used as a tether for the bungee cord the Borrowers needed to scale the kitchen counter to borrow some salt?

Perhaps. •

Patricia Joslin lives in Charlotte NC. Her essays have appeared in the *Personal Story Publishing Project—That Southern Thing, 2020, Luck and Opportunity*, 2021. Her poems are included in the *Kakalak*, 2021 and 2022 anthologies. Patricia's poem, "Today at Low Tide," was selected by the NC Poetry Society for its 2023 "Poetry in Plain Sight" poster program. Her chapbook, *I'll Buy Flowers Again Tomorrow*, a collection of poems about loss and healing, will be published in 2023 by Charlotte Lit Press. When not writing she works to improve her golf game.

Holding Hands

by Karen Sleeth

Momma was lovely. Not the hair-curled, made-up, high-heeled lovely but the head thrown back and laughing, let's play hide-n-seek, look at these ants carrying a stick kind of lovely. She was curious, and she noticed life. Mostly what I recognized—and coveted—was that she noticed me.

One day while my sister, Marsha, was at school, Momma took me into the backyard under a towering oak tree and presented a splendid picnic. I can't remember what we ate—probably peanut butter sandwiches, but I remember that she had poured my chocolate milk into a Pepsi bottle just like she and Daddy drank from. I was elated. I was a *big girl*. We were just two friends sharing a picnic and drinking our own Pepsis. I don't remember, but I'm sure I made Marsha jealous.

Momma and I had several excursions while Marsha was at school. I recall once going into a large department store and Momma insisting that I hold her hand. I squirmed out of her grasp several times, my attention drawn to something on a distant shelf. She would scold me and again take my hand.

I don't know how many times this happened but at one point when I had finished being enthralled by an item, I looked up to an aisle devoid of my Momma. I looked in both directions and no Momma. A coldness gripped my heart. I was alone. All alone.

"Momma?" I cried out. There was no answer.

"Mommmmmma?" Again, I pleaded, finally breaking into sobs. I sat on the lowest shelf and gave into the flood of tears so torrential that I was unable to see. After what seemed like hours and was probably minutes or seconds, a blurry figure squatted in front of me, wiping my wet face.

"You're okay," Momma said as I flung my arms around her neck. "Now don't let go of my hand, I don't want you to get lost."

A relief so intense swept through me that I resolved never to let go of her hand again no matter what appealed to me. Years later I overheard her say that she had been on the opposite aisle watching me the entire time.

I was reared in that *spare-the-rod-and-spoil-the-child* era when it was believed that any infraction or fault could be exorcized with a spanking. My inability to control my limbs as yet meant I was often the recipient of the un-spared rod. At one weekend lunch I recall Momma flitting around the table and telling Marsha and me, though I knew it was addressed to me: "*The first one who spills her milk is getting a spanking.*" Not an appetite

inducement for a then 5-year-old, I was afraid
to reach for my grilled cheese sandwich. But sitting with my
hands clasping each other in my lap, as I recall it, I still heard
the too familiar and dreaded *clunk*. I watched the white liquid
spread across the table. Wide eyed, I looked at Momma.
Marsha began to giggle. Momma smiled and made her
pronouncement again: "The first one who spills the milk gets
a spanking." She reached around and spanked herself to our
squeals and delighted laughter.

I held Momma's hand the day Marsha and I took her to the
nursing home. I feared that she would plant her feet in the
lobby, put her hands on her hips, and demand to know what
was going on. I still clung to the notion that her active mind
was in there, even though the week before at a medical evalu-
ation she did not know who I was, and more startling she did
not know her own name. We walked her to the room assigned
to her, and I went to the admissions office to complete the
paperwork. Marsha told me afterward that Momma ate the
lunch they had provided, and then quietly crawled into bed and
went to sleep. When I got to her room, I touched her shoulder,
which roused her a bit. She looked at me.

"We are leaving now, Momma," I said.

She smiled and said, "Ok," and went back to sleep.

During her first couple of months at the nursing home,
Momma caused a bit of a stir. She persisted in going to other
people's rooms and holding their hands. A few residents did

not like it, but true to form that did not stop Momma. I have not been able to touch her mind, heart, or memory in years, but I can still hold her hand. She always grasps mine as if I am still 5.

For now, holding hands with Momma keeps us both from getting lost. •

Karen Sleeth lives in Durham, North Carolina. She is a member of the North Carolina Writers Network and the Renegade Writers Group. Her work has appeared or is forthcoming in *The Main Street Rag, Potato Soup Journal, 2022 Best of Potato Soup Journal, Café Lit Magazine,* and others. Currently she is attending Lindenwood University in St. Charles, Missouri. She will complete an MFA in Creative Writing in May of 2023.

Tea with the Queen
by Kay Harper Windsor

Elizabeth sat between her two older brothers. She was mostly elbows, sitting stiffly and at the ready to push them back into their spaces and keep hers if they dared lean so much as an inch toward her. The three shared a bench seat in the back of our station wagon on the eight-hour trip to Ocracoke Island on the Outer Banks.

To pass the time in the car, the three children and I would read together. We had brought books, Roald Dahl's *BFG* (Big Friendly Giant) among them. The brothers liked Dahl's quirky humor, and in that particular book, I liked the idea that a "giant" offered Sophie, a young orphan girl, protection against fearful night dreams.

When my daughter awoke from bad dreams at home, I would move my fingers over her eyelids to whisper them closed as we talked of hopes to come in the morning light: daffodils waving, sun winking through the trees, library trips, following her brothers on their bikes as she rode her Strawberry Shortcake tricycle, hikes with brothers and Skipper the beagle— all images for good dreams to chase away the bad ones.

I needed those dreams too, lost to good dreams as I was for a time, longing for that daughter lost to us at 15.

As I read Dahl's *BFG* on that trip to Ocracoke to the children—5, 7, and 10 years old—the story was engaging enough to relax Elizabeth's elbows and lulling enough to allow one brother to sketch and the other to play chess. Elizabeth picked up on unusual details in the story.

"Wait! Did Sophie really come to the Queen's bedroom? And the Queen helped the BFG?!"

A little later, she continued: "What's the Queen of England's whole name?" and "Her name is the same as mine!" Finally, "Do you think the Queen of England would come to my room to keep away bad dreams?"

"Dreams," the Big Friendly Giant said in Dahl's book, "is very mysterious things. They is floating around in the air like little wispy-misty bubbles. And all the time they is searching for sleeping people."

We did not talk about *BFG* and scary dreams anymore until we were back home in our log house in the woods in Tobaccoville, North Carolina.

Blowing bubbles on the porch one day, Elizabeth said she was blowing away bad dreams. And after watching the wedding of one of Queen Elizabeth's sons on TV, she asked about the BFG and the Queen. "Can I write her a letter and ask her if Sophie really sat on a windowsill in her bedroom? And can

I tell her I saw her son's wedding and ask if she knows the BFG?"

We researched the mailing address and the proper salutation and closing for a letter to the Queen. We included Elizabeth's drawing of the wedding with the letter, and Elizabeth offered to Queen Elizabeth that if she ever came to North Carolina, she should please come to her house for tea. She added: "Do you know that you have the same name I have: Elizabeth Windsor?"

Weeks later we received an envelope with a red seal. Elizabeth had a handwritten letter (with "real ink," she noted) from a Lady in Waiting of Queen Elizabeth II. Her Majesty had directed that the Lady in Waiting thank Elizabeth for the drawing and for her letter.

Some 20 years after our Elizabeth died, during passing of the peace in church one morning, a friend told me that her son, who was in Elizabeth's first grade class, still remembered her bringing that letter from the Queen for *Show and Tell*.

Searching through old school papers, I found the letter again and remembered our reading Roald Dahl. I smiled at the memory of my daughter who feared and faced bad dreams and was comforted by a story where a powerful queen helped chase away unfriendly giants who blew bad dreams in through windows, comforted too by a "real" letter from a queen who took time to respond to a child who lived in the woods of North Carolina, almost 4,000 miles from Windsor Castle.

Tea with the Queen

One Elizabeth Windsor lived to be 96 years old in 2022, and one Elizabeth Windsor lived to age 15 in 1996. They shared a name; they exchanged letters; they never shared tea. But perhaps through the "wispy-misty bubbles" that are dreams, the two Elizabeth Windsors have now found conversation beyond exchanging letters and over tea.

Those two brothers have now soothed both bad dreams and seating placement on long car trips for their own families, and I have brought the remembrance of Elizabeth's letter to tea party conversations with my grandchildren, Elizabeth's nieces and nephew. She just may have passed to them some of her spirited curiosity and spunk. •

Kay Harper Windsor leads reflective writing sessions for Trellis Supportive Care in Winston-Salem and for community groups. She served as a national mentor for journalism teachers after four decades of teaching. For 20 years, she has been part of the Farther Along writing group, and her writing is included in *Farther Along: The Writing Journey of Thirteen Bereaved Mothers* and at fartheralongbook.com.

Kay is a mother of three children and a grandmother of seven grandchildren, all storytellers. Writing friend and story catcher Susan encouraged Kay to share this story.

A Fine Work

by Joe Brown

I cleaned up my truck last week. It was time. The fall weather was getting cooler, and I had a 3-day weekend. It took all three days. It had been years since I had taken on the task and the large tray behind the seats had begun to overflow with stuff. My first task on Friday was to clean out everything in the cab and to vacuum the cracks and crevices, the carpet and seats. While removing the clothes and forgotten tools, getting up the petrified trail mix, and a host of other lost items, I found a story about my mother. I had penciled it during my watch, while my two brothers, my sister, and I were taking turns staying nights with Mom in the waning days of her life. Here is the most valuable thing I found in my truck.

Busy Hands
December 13, 2014, 3:20 a.m.
According to the Corporate World a successful woman strives to attain rank and climb the Corporate Ladder, make lots of money and be important in the eyes of others. My Mother did not work at these things! She didn't go to "work"; shucks, she is one of a handful of people that I know that never had a driver's license. She tried driving a couple of times, but it just wasn't for her.

Mom's hands did find things to do though. She was a good field hand. Mom would follow Papa George (Dad), dropping tobacco plants into the old water-filled, handheld tobacco setter. Her hands would drop single plants, at just the right time, all day long or until the job was done. Later in the season at Priming Time, she would tie hand after hand of tobacco leaves onto sticks with white string. Stick after stick until all the sleds were empty. She tied many a barn of tobacco. She did this season after season for most of her life. Our Family and surrounding neighbors could count on Mom's Hands to help put in the crop.

Of course, it wasn't just tobacco fields, but acre after acre of "Truck crops," just called gardens. We had the Creek bottom Garden, the River Bottom Garden, the Hillside Garden, you get the picture? We raised them for trade, to sell, and for the family Table. Mom said there were two things she didn't need in the garden—Kids and Dogs. She did most of the hoeing, weeding, and picking herself.

After the harvesting there was the preparation, canning, freezing or cooking, so it could be eaten either now or later. Mom's hands knew just how to do all that also.

She was also a seamstress; people would come to her for a new Dress or other articles of clothing to be made, adjusted, or mended. She loved to embroider and cross stitch. In the winter, when it was cold outside, she would "piece" together little squares and make a quilt or two, teaching other family members the best way to do this or that.

When they were biting or the baskets in the river caught a good mess of catfish, Papa George and us boys might bring in a couple hundred or more. Did you know Mom would set up way into the night, cleaning, and packaging and freezing them? Yes, her hands could really clean catfish!

Boy, was Mom also a good country cook? She always put good food on the table, even when times were hard. Some of our favorites were Fried catfish, Turtle Stew, Squirrel Gravy and Biscuits, Quail Pie, Roasted possum or Coon and always a favorite, Persimmon Pudding. Of course, she used a lot of fresh squeezed whole milk from the Family cow; yes, she did the milking too. Her hands knew how to do all that and much more.

Among other things that her hands were busy at, were keeping up with the family bills, keeping house, raising Kids, Grandkids when needed, and helping with the Flowers and other things at Church.

Mom was the family Historian. If you needed to know who married who and when, Mom remembered. Which side of the family did cousin so-and-so belong to? Mom knew.

So maybe Faye Brown did not strive to be a "Big Wig Executive," but her hands did good works after all.

She always had Busy—and in my mind successful—Hands!

But what made me think of all the things my mother's hands did is that tonight Mom's hands struggle for hours with the

A Fine Work

hems of the sheets, like some unsolvable puzzle.
Mom's "Busy Hands" did a fine work, no doubt about it.

———————————

I was happy to recover that penciled letter from the refuse
"stored away" in my truck, especially because Mom had gone
home to be with her Lord and Papa George two days after
I wrote it.

Exhaustion and heightened emotions can flow right out when
we write them down. Those words can be a blessing to you
and others when you rediscover them. •

Copyright 2023, Joe Brown

Joseph Brown is a native of North Carolina, born in Yadkin County
and reared in Davie County. He now resides in the Bethania area of
Forsyth County and has lived all his life within 40 miles of his birth-
place. In February 2020 he retired from 50 years in the construction
industry. Most of his previous writing has been daily journals on his
mission trips to Kentucky, Canada, and Ecuador. His earliest
published stories appeared in 2019, 2020, and 2021 Personal Story
Publishing Projects.

Editor's note: Another version of this story appeared previously on
"6-minute Stories" podcast as a bonus episode during Season 2, in
May 2020.

Love Never Dies

by Phyllis Castelli

"Gracie was more like an angel of compassion than an actual dog," whispered Maria, sipping her coffee. "A piece of my heart is gone." I nodded silently, comforted by the sympathy. I am not new to grief and will someday heal, but the bruises from this sudden death will be tender for a long time.

When Gracie died, the days that followed were faded and bleak, as if light and color were bereft without her. My heart echoed singer Fiona Apple's words, "My dog has stopped being a dog and is now part of everything. She is in the wind, and in the soil, and the snow, and in me, wherever I go." I wrap that insight around myself like a snuggly sweater. My sweet girl will always be with me, deep in the marrow of my being.

A beautiful Black Labrador Retriever, Gracie joyfully wallowed in life as a delightful gift. She loved all things doggie: dirt, the zoomies, yellow tennis balls, and squeaky duck toys. A naughty foodaholic, she raided the kitchen trash can and gobbled up random stuff from the yard.

Gracie frequently went with me to church and happily played a role in the Children's Sermons. She greeted friends in the pews, listened to the preacher, and watched the congregation with her peaceful, steady gaze, perhaps wondering why we bumbling humans struggle so hard to find our way. Gracie knew that love was the answer to every question and had unwavering faith in the goodness of creation.

Shortly after Gracie's eighth birthday, I found on her a large mast cell tumor that required removal. The extensive surgery was successful, with an excellent prognosis. Life returned to normal, happy and playful.

Then, like suddenly landing in an upside-down universe, my dog could not breathe. We rushed to the veterinary specialty hospital, an hour away. The doctors there found a new, fast-growing tumor bleeding into Gracie's chest, hurrying to take her life by stealing her breath. They gave her mere hours to live. She was panting but calm and untroubled.

Devastated and running out of time, I made arrangements to take the next heartbreaking step with our beloved veterinarian, Dr. Bridget Waters. My younger dog, Oliver, was with us. He needed to know for himself that Sissy was gone. Dr. Waters mercifully euthanized my sweet girl, ensuring she would not die terrified and gasping for breath. I held Gracie close, loved and talked to her until, like a whisper in the wind, she was gone.

For a moment, I sat in stunned silence, followed by the blank static of the drive home. I unlocked the door. Oliver and I went inside. Grief poured over us like a river, like the very earth was weeping.

Gracie lived and died surrounded by love and joy. She never knew how sick she was and thus was not afraid. Death was but one part of her journey, a devastating but expected end to a whole life.

Grief has moved into our house and will be there for a while. Grief is not something we carry around voluntarily, like glasses or car keys. We sort of move along with grief, keeping pace on some days and running ahead on others, but it never becomes an easy companion.

Oliver and I learned a different way to be in the world, working around the abyss of Gracie's absence. I took him with me everywhere. Life was okay, but nothing was fun. He could not play, and our world seemed permanently stifling and stagnant. I longed to feel Gracie's fur and have her within arm's reach. I needed to see her attentive face and missed the soft snuffle of her sleeping on my pillow. Without a big sister for the first time, Oliver grew listless. Gracie had been full of mischief and playful energy, the bringer of joy. We were sad, empty.

Today, a mix of midday sun and shadows drifts across our yard. Oliver sits tall in a deck chair, tail wagging. In his mouth is a colorful caterpillar toy held high. At his feet, bright toys and squeaky balls are strewn helter-skelter, and a barking, dancing Labrador puppy is leaping full throttle to re-capture her favorite toy. Oliver has fallen in love with little Cara, who is feisty, exuberant, and wholly herself.

When we commit to caring for an animal biologically destined to die before we do, we invite inevitable pain into our lives. However, there is boundless joy in choosing love anyway, along with a conscious appreciation of every messy, irrepressible moment. Grief will always have a place at the bountiful table of life, so I also take my seat, lay my napkin in my lap, and have another helping when I have to because I know that love never dies. •

Phyllis Castelli returned home to Henderson, North Carolina, after retiring from her music career. She spends time with her lifetime special interests: writing, music, photography, a pollinator garden, and Black Labrador Retrievers. Phyllis loves to create projects that knit together the beauty of those favorites. Phyllis's poems and essays have appeared in *Quillkeepers Press, The Avocet, Scarlet Leaf Review*, and *Tar River Poets*, among others. As a child poet, she published *Gentle, I Think*, a book of poems with pen and ink illustrations.

Up the Creek
by Howard Pearre

The bad news was we lost our paddles. The good news was we had strapped those stiff orange life vests on our chests, rather than just tossing them in the boat.

Ray and I were in our late 20s and had enjoyed canoe riding on the Yadkin and on a few gentle streams in Wilkes County. This'll be a hoot! we thought.

Along with a dozen or so other paddlers, we lined up for the start of the first annual New River Canoe Race near the put-in point a few miles north of Sparta. The course would take us about five miles, bending into Grayson County, Virginia, then back into North Carolina.

The river was "up" from a week of heavy rain. Some competitors expressed concern, but we thought otherwise. It still would be only three or four feet deep, we would not be annoyed by getting stuck in shallow areas, and if the worst happened, we'd just stand up, pour out the water, and climb back in.

We had no idea about how extra water can affect the force of a river's current. We had no idea about the consequences of that current slamming a 15-foot piece of molded fiberglass against one of the thousands of boulders that litter the New. We had no idea how much heavier our 70-pound canoe would be when filled with water. And we had no idea about the deep holes that were hidden in quiet places along the course.

The gun sounded. Ray and I dug our paddles into the water, more interested in powering ahead than performing any fine technical skills required to navigate the swift-flowing river.

A minute into the race, we were tied for the lead with one other canoe. A minute-and-a-half later, the fierce current grabbed our boat, turned it sideways, and bashed it against a boulder the size of a washing machine.

Water poured over the edge of the canoe, filling and submerging it. Ray and I fell out. We attempted to stand in four feet of water, but the ferocious current pushed our bodies toward Virginia. Our gear and paddles sailed away. The canoe swung around the boulder, rolled over, and followed the disappearing gear. I grabbed the rope attached to one end of the canoe with one hand while frantically holding my glasses in place with the other.

I struggled to swim out of the current toward a bank while holding the rope, and, after several minutes, was able to pull the canoe into a quiet pool. We reached the steep bank of mud, brush, briars, and small trees. After scrambling onto a narrow perch, I tied the rope to a tree. We sat for the next ten minutes, catching our breaths. Utterly shaken, we assessed the scratches and bruises that adorned our legs and arms. In front of us was the river, churning wildly. Behind us was steep terrain as far as I could see. The terrain beyond the other bank was just as steep and formidable.

One of the canoe's air-pocket ends apparently had been damaged and had filled with water. The end that had endured the crash was sticking out of the water so that only a foot of the canoe was visible. The rest was submerged—vertically.

With the little strength we had left, we pulled the canoe out of the deep hole and picked up one side to spill water out the other. There were ugly scars and gashes on both sides.

Another canoe rider, paddling solo—and who had not been hell-bent on taking the lead—appeared. He asked if we were okay. We said we'd cracked up on a boulder, that our canoe was badly damaged, and we had lost our paddles. He had an extra and loaned it to us. He also asked us if we needed something to bail out water and gave us a plastic drink cup.

We completed the racecourse only because there was no other way out. For the rest of the trip, we hugged the bank, used the plastic cup to bail incoming water, and watched a carefree group of tubers splashing and laughing as they bounced off the giant rocks.

The next week, I made my regular trip to Sparta to follow up with some clients. I stopped for lunch at the town's drug store that also had a snack bar. Standing in a corner next to crutches and orthopedic supplies, were my paddles, with a few more scars than I remembered. The manager said one of the race participants had rescued them and left them there in case the owner might come by.

"Yes," I said sheepishly. "They're mine." •

Howard Pearre's fiction and memoir stories have appeared in Personal Story Publishing Project anthologies, *Flying South*, *GreenPrints*, and *The Dead Mule School of Southern Literature*. His short story "September, 1957" received an honorable mention at the 2020 International Human Rights Arts Festival. He also writes articles promoting voting for the Winston-Salem Chronicle and is a board member of Winston-Salem Writers. He retired after a career as a counselor and manager with NC Vocational Rehabilitation and the US Department of Veterans Affairs.

The Blessing of Unanswered Prayers
by Gene Hoots

The energy business was the place to be in the 1970s. Oil prices increased more than ten-fold. Media, citing the usual "experts," reported that in only a few decades the world would run out of oil. Unless the world found more oil, civilization was doomed. Finding and producing this "black gold" was the business to be in. You could be part of saving the world! Petroleum companies were advertising for workers on billboards and radio, offering signing bonuses for those willing to jump ship from a current employer. Cities that had energy companies were booming. If people had a home to sell in Houston, they just stuck a "For Sale" sign in their yard, and most houses sold in less than three days. Oil prices were going to rise forever, and prospects were bright.

In 1975 I got connected to the "oil patch" and bought into the oil-boom enthusiasm. My employer, R.J. Reynolds Tobacco Company, was considering a rather odd investment—an oil company. It would be the biggest acquisition ever at that time. But more exciting for me would be a job in Houston, and I fantasized about becoming a "Texas oil man." I spent 14 months in New York, Dallas, and Houston. My wife willingly made the effort to run our family with no help. But, after all that time away from home in North Carolina, the oil company boss in New York told me there was no job for me in Houston. Major organizational changes had made many of the jobs there "redundant."

I packed my bag, caught a train in New York City, and headed south. My head was down, and my tail was tucked between my legs. It was a long, sad trip, a bitter pill to swallow. More than a year had been invested in trying to reach a goal that was never going to happen.

Back home, I busied myself with routine tasks at the office. On my own time, I began to work on a small stock investment partnership. One of the people who oversaw the oil project was the RJR Treasurer. A few months after coming home, he asked if I would manage the RJR pension fund. I accepted, thinking it would be a short-term assignment. My qualifications were minimal, hardly more than some small experience analyzing stocks. But that was enough. A Greek proverb says, "Among the blind, the one-eyed is king." And in a cigarette company, my limited experience was still enough to make me a "king" compared to most other job candidates. And most of them would not want the job anyway. Running the pension did not look like a job with great promise, but at least it would keep me on the payroll.

For the next ten years, all the "experts" were wrong, as they often are. Yogi Berra said, "It's tough to make predictions, especially about the future." Oil prices crashed in 1980. The energy industry entered a steep decline, taking years to recover. In Houston, I would have been inexperienced, with no prospects, and no job network. Petroleum companies fired thousands of employees.

The oil crisis passed, but oil has steadily become a smaller part of the U.S. economy. In contrast, employee savings and investing grew rapidly in America. The pension market was the fastest growing segment of that industry, and RJR was a part of that. Its retirement assets grew, in a decade, from a small fund in America to 20 times the original size, in 27 countries.

Luck put me in one of the great growth industries of the last 45 years. And all because the job I desperately wanted did not materialize. That lucky break sent me down a path that I never expected. RJR gave me invaluable on-the-job training. Leaving RJR in 1986, I co-founded an investment company and worked there for 32 years. Personally rewarding, it was an opportunity to help people secure a better financial future and to build scores of new friendships that have lasted a lifetime—work that continues part-time even today.

Now, it is easy to see that the day my Texas "dream" was crushed, leaving me with an uncertain future and real disappointment, was one of the best days of my life.

It is sometimes a blessing that our prayers go unanswered. We do not always have enough wisdom to ask for the right things. •

The Blessing of Unanswered Prayers

Gene Hoots, a Winston-Salem native, lived in the nearby farming area before moving to Charlotte in 1996. He wrote *Pay Attention to the Thin Cow*, a collection of essays on life experiences in 2012, and *Going Down Tobacco Road*, a history of the tobacco industry and R.J. Reynolds Tobacco Company in 2020. His trip down Tobacco Road has been enriched with friendships and experiences that he could never have imagined when he started his journey back in 1939. He has worked 60 years in financial analysis and investing.

The Essentials

by Catherine Parisio

"Catherine, get out here, NOW!"

The urgency in my husband's voice was unmistakable. My heart seized up and I bolted from the sink without even thinking. Wiping my hands on my shirt, I ran out from the restroom.

"Watch these!" Pier shouted, throwing two large backpacks at my feet. Confusion took hold as I watched him vanish into the crowd.

Moments later I spotted him pushing through the main doors of the La Paz bus station. He beelined towards me, his eyes revealing a mix of fear and anger.

"Somebody stole our backpack."

"Oh, shit." I slumped onto the bench, realizing our passports were in that bag. Our bus to Cusco, Peru, was leaving momentarily, but without passports, we could not board. And it was

not just the passports. Everything essential was in that bag—
our credit cards, ATM card, and more than a month's salary
in cash. My stomach clenched at the thought of all our
vacation money gone.

Pier went to the ticket agent. Thankfully, she was sympathetic
and refunded our money, providing us with at least some
funds.

"How could we have been so stupid?"

I knew what Pier meant. We knew the risk of putting everything important in one bag, but we had been out late
celebrating with friends, and packing was a low priority. I had
planned to repack at the bus station, but in the early morning
fogginess of too much wine and too little sleep, I just didn't do
it.

"What do we do now?" I wondered aloud.

We talked about catching the bus back to Cochabamba and our
apartment, but that felt like defeat. We had a month-long trip
planned and we had been gone for only 18 hours. We were not
going to let the thieves steal our vacation as well.

We made arrangements to get new passports and have some
money wired. With nothing more to do for the moment, we
found a cheap room for the night. In silence, we crawled onto
the bed and huddled together. No amount of tears or swearing
was going to bring back our bag, so once we calmed our
emotions, we revised our travel plans to reflect our new reality.

In the morning we headed to the nearby town of Sorata. Boarding the bus, I marveled at the *cholitas* who managed to carry everything they needed wrapped in a blanket slung across their shoulders—including their babies! The bustling chaos of Lima receded, and the bus was soon careening down the narrow dirt road that connects the Altiplano to the Yungas lowlands. Without a camera to capture the scenery, I focused on the small details of the landscape so I could later write precise descriptions in my journal. Peering out the window, I said a little prayer as I glimpsed the heart-stopping drop-offs that were entirely too close to the wheels of the bus. In the distance, the craggy, snow-covered peaks of Illampu burst out from the flat desert plain, a giant white creature hulking over the dusty expanse.

After several hours on the twisting road, Sorata came into view, a relief to my queasy stomach. The surrounding valley was a patchwork of family farms clinging to the steep hillsides. Sheep grazed on lush grass as farmers tended their fields with the simplest of tools, ones that I imagine had been used for generations. I settled back in my seat, truly savoring the moment; the sun, fresh air, and brilliant blue sky filling me with a deepening contentment.

As we stepped off the bus, a young man greeted us, offering us a room. Normally we would be reluctant to trust a stranger, but, given that our guidebook had been among the items stolen, we had a newfound appreciation for the kindness of strangers. He led us to his home. The available room was

simple, and the bathroom was shared, but it was clean, close
to the main plaza, and, best of all, less than the equivalent
of $5 per night.

During our altered vacation, we came to realize the items lost
in that stolen backpack were not indispensable after all. An
ability to adapt, to appreciate simplicity, and to recognize the
gifts that come from facing adversity are the important skills
for life. And the trip we created was an experience that
I would not have had otherwise. Hiking along the shores of
Lake Titicaca, soaking my feet in the hot springs of the Uyuni
Salt Flats, and crawling around the silver mines of Potosi are
memories that can never be taken away.

And, to prove that we really did not lose anything *essential* at all,
years later we lived and worked in Peru, where we visited all
the places we had originally planned to see during our "stolen"
vacation. •

Catherine Parisio spent nearly two decades living overseas and
teaching at international schools. From South America to Africa
to the Middle East, the insights and challenges of expat life, as well
as the wealth of travel opportunities available, give her a lot to write
about. Living in Oregon at present, she and her husband are
adjusting to life as empty-nesters and are eager for their next
adventure. When she is not out on the trail with her hiking buddies,
Catherine works as a freelance book editor and she writes.

Historic Preservation
Goes off the Rails

by Harry Enoch

My story is not about a great loss but more of a big disappointment. While residing in Clark County, Kentucky, for the last 23 years, I've become involved in research and writing about the people, places, and events that shaped our local history. This led quite naturally to an interest in historic preservation. The county has many historic buildings worthy of saving, and we can count a number of successes in rescuing endangered structures. In Winchester we mark the largely intact downtown business area as win-win for everyone. The number of buildings purchased and rehabilitated over the last few years has now reached double digits and continues unabated. The scorecard, however, does reflect a few failures and one in particular—sadly for me personally—restoring the V.W. Bush Warehouse, better known as the "Sphar Building."

The building, erected in 1880 by Valentine White Bush, served as the first railway warehouse in Winchester. His two-story brick facility stood on North Main Street beside the Elizabethtown, Lexington & Big Sandy Railroad (later the C&O), near the passenger depot. Business was better than good at the warehouse. Over the years, they purchased, processed, and stored a variety of agricultural products, which could be conveniently shipped to markets by rail. Hemp and bluegrass seed fueled profits for over a century, and then in the mid-1900s the Sphar family operated a lucrative business selling feed and seed. By the time the last business closed in 2005, the building was showing its age. Though solidly built of heavy oak timbers, a leaking roof had compromised several of the load-bearing walls.

Preservation efforts began to pay off a decade later. City and county government finally recognized the importance of saving this landmark, the last original building still standing on the north end of Main Street. A plan emerged to use the restored structure to house two local agencies—Tourism and Industrial Development—as well as the Chamber of Commerce and another nonprofit group. It would function as the city's welcome center and would have a small museum. The city purchased the old warehouse in 2016. To fund restoration work, $1.9 million was raised from grants and pledges. My involvement began with a request that September to prepare the nomination of the building for the National Register. That designation would allow tax credits of up to 20 percent of the rehabilitation costs.

These nominations are usually prepared by specialty consultants who typically charge up to $10,000 and take six to 12 months. I had no previous experience, the nomination had to be completed in 30 days, and no funds were available to pay for my work. I buried myself in the task to the exclusion of all else and finished before the deadline. Kentucky Heritage Council approved the nomination and submitted it to the

National Park Service, who listed the property on the National Register of Historic Places in March 2017.

The restoration process began with a condition assessment by the architect-engineering firm. They identified several problem areas: a partly collapsed north wall due to failure of the roof system, part of the east wall in bad shape, and a number of floor joists rotted due to water damage. Exterior walls on the north and east facade had damaged bricks that needed repair, and much of the brick work needed tuck pointing. They estimated restoration costs at approximately $2 million. With the grants, pledges, and tax credits, this seemed a promising beginning.

When the actual construction bids were opened, the low bid was $2.9 million. Rather than seeking additional funding or modifying plans, the city commission simply voted to end their involvement in the project. I joined other preservation activists in efforts to save the building. It seemed quite feasible at that time to stabilize the building with the available funds and then complete fitting out the interior spaces when more funds became available.

From that point on, the project suffered one disaster after another. After the county voted to return a community block grant of $500,000, one of the nonprofit organizations backed out. Cost estimates for even a scaled-back project exceeded available funds. The final insult came with a major roof collapse (The city had made no effort to prevent further water damage during the time it owned the building). The Sphar Building was razed in January 2020.

Historic Preservation Goes off the Rails

In the early 1900s Winchester was considered a railroad town. Our community then counted over 20 passenger trains a day. Passenger service ended in 1971. In 1981 the railroad demolished Union Station, then pulled their tracks up in 1990. The landmark warehouse represented our last tie to a thriving rail-related industry that helped make Winchester what it became. I never drive by the site without recalling the pain associated with its loss. •

Harry Enoch is a native Mt. Sterling, Kentucky, and graduate of the University of Kentucky (B.S., PhD). He has lived in Clark County since 1999 and has a passion for the past. He has researched, written, and published extensively about the history of this area. Books include *In Search of Morgan's Station and "The Last Indian Raid in Kentucky," Captain Billy Bush and the Bush Settlement, Colonel John Holder: Boonesborough Defender & Kentucky Entrepreneur, Women at Fort Boonesborough,* and *African Americans at Fort Boonesborough.*

Blue Light Blues
by Patricia E. Watts

A t 16, I had passed my Driver's Ed course, complete with perfect parallel parking on our very busy Main Street. Not only was I awarded my driver's license, but I also got the long-awaited keys to the green and white '55 Pontiac. Life was good!

Two weeks later I was happily running an errand. When I got to the bottom of our street and turned the corner, my transistor radio slid off the passenger's seat and landed on the floorboards with a thud. I bent down to retrieve it and when I looked up, it was too late. I centered a light pole on the corner. I sat a moment trying to decide what to do next. Then I thought, *If I don't tell my dad, the neighbors certainly will!* So, I backed up and headed down to his establishment. He told me to go back to the scene of the accident and he would be there shortly. I waited patiently only to see he had a police car following him. The officer asked for an explanation and after giving him the details, my dad asked him to write me a moving violation ticket, one that required me to come before the judge in traffic court. The officer handed me my ticket and my dad told me to follow him home. When he got out of his car at our house, he pulled a piece of paper from his wallet and wrote down the mileage on the odometer of the Pontiac. He then asked for my keys and driver's license. He said I could sit in my car if I wanted or I could wash it, but I couldn't drive it for six weeks. That meant that in two weeks flat I had lost my driver's license.

To add insult to injury it also meant I now had to resume once again walking the one-and-a-half miles each way to my high school.

My court day came, and dad drove me to the courthouse. When the Judge called me forward, he, too, asked for an explanation which I once again offered.

"Whose car were you driving?" the judge asked.

"Mine," I answered.

"Is it in your name?"

"Yes, sir. I earned it babysitting."

The judge paused for a long time. He said he did not think babysitting paid enough to buy a car. So, I explained. "To earn it, I had to babysit my younger brother every day after school, every Saturday, and every summer for three years straight while my parents worked.

The judge offered another long pause. I don't think he quite knew what to do with me. Then he asked if I had learned anything from this experience.

"Yes, sir. Two lessons. One was not to leave the scene of an accident. And the other one was never to buy a car without a radio in it." I could hear laughter in the courtroom behind me.

The judge then tore up my ticket and said I could go but he did not want to see me back in his courtroom again.

The drive home was completely silent. When we arrived, my dad pulled the piece of paper out of his wallet to verify that the odometer reading in the Pontiac had not changed and then he handed me my keys and driver's license. And he gave me a big ole' bear hug.

Fifteen years later I was the legal secretary for the City Attorney. I was sitting at a red light behind two other vehicles when *WHAM*, the car behind me rammed me into the two cars in front of me. When I looked in the rearview mirror and saw it was a police car, I swallowed hard. My first thought was *I bet they will blame me!* And the second thought was, *Oh, goodness, if this goes to court my boss will have to defend the policeman against me!* That could not be good! About that time the officer ran up to my window and said, "It's all cut and dried! It's all my fault. I wasn't watching where I was going!"

We were only three blocks from the police station, so it did not take the Police Chief long to get to the scene. With his face beet red, he slammed his fist down on the fender of the crumpled patrol car and yelled, "Doggone it, this is a brand-new car! We haven't even had it a week!"

Blue Light Blues

I thought I might suggest to the Chief that he could take the policeman's license for six weeks and make him walk to work. And he could certainly ask him what he had learned from this! But I didn't say anything. I was just glad I did not have to go to court.

So, that's why I just gave the policeman a big ole' bear hug. •

Patricia E. Watts lives in Mountville, South Carolina where the love of local and family history has given her a passion to write stories to pass down to her children. She has found through stories of tragedies, tears, and triumphs and even mysteries that she has a rich heritage worth telling. Six stories have appeared in previous PSPP anthologies: "A Real Small Town," the paired stories "Sometimes the Prize Goes to the Wrong Person" and "The Orphan Train," "Chancing the Buddy System," "The Class of '44 Ring," and "The Saltwater Taffy Escapade."

Finding Home
by J.P. McGillicuddy

While rummaging through my attic, I came upon my 1975 high school yearbook. Along with photos of my senior-year classmates, this almanac contained each person's remembrances and aspirations. Under my stoic mugshot, I declared my future plans were "to be happy."

In reality, my only ambition was to escape my childhood home and never to return, a singular goal born from years of parental violence heaped upon me and my five sisters. At the time, my notion of happiness was freedom from physical abuse.

Following the example of my four older sisters, I secured a student loan and enrolled at the University of Massachusetts. During two aimless years at UMASS, I searched for happiness as if it were found at the bottom of a beer keg. Only when UMASS placed me on probation did I sober up to the reality of being utterly lost about my future. I'd escaped the terror of my parents' violence but happiness remained enigmatic.

I only felt happy when playing sports, which served as a refuge from the rest of my life. I could shut out the world and just be me. Although I was an all-star high school athlete, I wasn't

talented enough to play professionally. But UMASS offered a
new major called Sports Management, including a track special-
izing in the business of professional sports. The prospect of
working in pro sports stimulated my first career aspiration—
becoming a general manager overseeing a sports franchise.

Despite never playing soccer, I decided to pursue my newfound ambition in this sport. I figured there would be less
competition for jobs in this new but growing game in the U.S.
However, the only job offer I received was with the Carolina
Lightnin', an American Soccer League (ASL) expansion
franchise in Charlotte, North Carolina. My three years with the
Lightnin' provided a wide array of experience. But the work
I fell in love with was writing and producing weekly game
magazines.

Although the Lightnin' won the ASL Championship in its first
year and led the league in attendance each season, the franchise
folded in 1983 when the ASL ceased operations, as did the
North American Soccer League, the only other outdoor pro
soccer league in the U.S. With no major league sports in
Charlotte, I sent feelers to pro teams in other cities. However,
something also tugged at me to stay.

Upon arriving in Charlotte, I'd joined an adult recreational
soccer league to familiarize myself with the sport. Soon,
playing soccer led to my developing friendships. It wasn't long
before I was managing a team of friends in the league.
Eventually, I served as league president. I had planted roots in
the community and was reluctant to sever these new relationships and have to start over somewhere else. So, I stayed

in Charlotte and shifted my career aims toward writing.

I spent the next five years producing brochures and newsletters for healthcare organizations, while writing freelance sports articles for a weekly newspaper. Eventually, this combination of experiences led to a job as the managing editor of a monthly magazine. Thrilled to be writing and editing full-time, as well as overseeing the entire publication, I had found my dream job.

Two years later this dream evaporated when the publisher relocated the company—but not the staff—to Rhode Island. Facing unemployment, I took a position with Mecklenburg County government as a public information specialist, serving as editor of the monthly employee magazine. Although grateful to be employed, I planned to return to publishing within 24 months. Instead, I spent 23 years with Mecklenburg County, being promoted twice before retiring in 2013 as Assistant County Manager, where I oversaw all business functions for this $2 billion organization.

Although I continued writing as part of my new responsibilities, County Manager Harry Jones, who promoted me to this senior executive position, deftly mentored me in servant leadership. He taught me the value and privilege of improving the community and the lives of its residents, while supporting and developing Mecklenburg County employees. Realizing this responsibility was more important and more rewarding than any personal ambition, I discovered new meaning to my work and my true dream job.

Like a pebble rolling down rocky terrain, my life has ricocheted in unpredictable directions. Despite making choices along the way, these random bounces made the difference. I never became a pro sports general manager. However, coming to Charlotte and the Carolina Lightnin' began a journey that led me to a love of writing, a rewarding career helping others, and fulfilling life-long relationships, including with my wife, Jenny. Together, she and I built a family and a life in the city where I found that home, and happiness found me.

Incidentally, when Harry Jones promoted me, the position title was "General Manager." So, yeah, I got there after all. •

J.P. McGillicuddy lives in Charlotte, North Carolina. A former magazine editor, he has authored numerous published articles spanning sports, health care and government. He also created and wrote "The Mecklenburgers," an award-winning local television program. His poetry received a 2019 award from Charlotte Writers Club and was exhibited in Mooresville Arts "Beyond Poems and Paintings" in 2020. His essays, "The White Section," "Opportunity Named Harry," "The Terror Inside" and "Eleven Eleven" appeared in previous anthologies of the Personal Story Publishing Project. He is a member of Charlotte Writers Club and NC Poetry Society.

A Terrible Way To Live
by Phyliss Grady Adcock

It was late summer 1968. A naive bride stood at the end of an aisle with her father, surrounded by brilliant stained-glass windows. At the other end was her high school sweetheart of seven years. The world was bright and shiny with many exciting adventures and possibilities. White lace, orchids, and sunshine made a perfect day for love and commitment.

Now that same bride stands alone in an ICU room looking at her once strong, athletic, ambitious sweetheart 40 years later. It is late summer 2008. He is no longer her husband. There is still sunshine and lots of white, but no orchids or possibilities. The adventure, for him, has reached its final destination.

He is unrecognizable—no suntanned face, no bright brown eyes, no thick hair, no muscular body, and no perfect smile. Instead, a whisper of a man is left on life support, antibiotics, bandages, and despair.

The bride is no longer naïve. The journey to this room has been different for the two occupants of this now sterile and hopeless place in time.

Their life after the wedding took them back to a college town to finish their senior years. She found the one thing she would always cling to no matter what, teaching. It would serve as a refuge, a place where she was loved, and the answer to her prayers. Teaching was where she was successful, where she was somebody.

He would begin his search for something, anything to feel special and really alive. He could not appreciate all the gifts he already had been given—a devoted wife, a loving sister, and later a beautiful daughter.

With all his plusses, athleticism, good looks, intelligence, and charisma came a terrible temper, dissatisfaction, cruelty, and self-centeredness. He was capable of flipping from complete euphoria to rage in a matter of seconds. It was predictably unpredictable. Violence was summoned and anyone could become prey. His favorite victim was the one who loved him most. She was the one who could forgive anything, endure everything, and bounce back with a sad smile hoping things would change. Change they did, but as every year passed things grew worse. Insults were more hurtful, more things were broken, and other women entered his reality. He loved new things, places, relationships, and career changes. But the new wore off quickly and the search continued for a better high. Corvettes, sports, staying out late, and a secret world which did not include his family, were all attempts to quench his insatiable desire for whatever.

Even the birth of his only child was a short-lived end-of-therainbow experience. She was the spitting image of her father, bright, loving, and humble. She was also a baby who needed her mother's attention and time, which he resented and fought to control. What a sad time for a new family. Everyone needed love and support in different ways. A mother was torn and scared, while an innocent baby did not understand. A father was determined to make everyone as miserable as he was. Days and nights become so long when there is no caring, kindness, or help. Tasks are completed, appearances are kept presentable, and souls are destroyed little by little. A brand-new life feels the stress and pain when cuddled in her mother's arms. That's not the emotion you want a gift from God to feel. She loved a mother who needed her as much as she needed her mother. *Who was clinging to whom?*

At the end of this 40-year journey he would leave a terrible legacy. Emotional damage was deep within the wife and daughter he once pretended to love. Both had gone on after he left, but the trauma of living in his world was always just below the surface.

His wife would find another to love, one who would not understand her defensiveness, but would spend his life trying to convince her that she was enough.

The beautiful baby would grow into an impressive young woman. She would also not feel enough and look for male validation and make some bad choices. She would find her Prince Charming eventually, one who made up for all the sadness and showed her how a real man loves.

A Terrible Way To Live

It seems we often take the wrong lessons from life. We become masters of survival techniques and forget to appreciate peace and joy, believing it may be only the calm before the storm. Being afraid of happiness is a terrible way to live.

I am that bride, of course, his favorite victim, and an exhausted breadwinner. I am now a determined survivor and the grateful, open-armed receiver of answered prayers. This is my story of dreadful, unwelcome heartache. This is my story of the triumph of the human spirit.

This is my story of what I lost and what I found. •

After teaching for 34 years, Phyliss Grady Adcock, retired in Morehead City, North Carolina. Her writing has appeared in *Mailbox Magazine*, *Teacher's Helper*, *That Southern Thing*, *Luck and Opportunity*, *Trouble*, and *Curious Stuff*. Her grant writing netted over $5,000 for classroom projects. For one grant proposal, she was recognized as the first Raychem Educator of the Year. She is listed in Who's Who Among America's Teachers for 1996 and 2000. She is currently writing humorous stories about the colorful characters in her family. Writing is her "Happy Place."

Tough Times
by Paula Teem Levi

In January 1883, my great-grandmother, Alsoney Horton, and her brother, Jefferson, were the only survivors from their family following a smallpox epidemic in Cincinnati, Ohio. The orphans were placed on a coal barge and sent upriver to live with relatives in Charleston, West Virginia.

Records from Alsoney's early life are scant, but the family stories suggest a determined and resourceful person who kept a low profile during difficult times.

A search of what records were available revealed a marriage record of Earl Cavender and Allie (Alsoney) Horton uniting in April 1920. Two years later, the City Directory for Charleston showed Allie and Earl on Fry Street with Earl employed as a farmer.

Earl, it seems, was working for some farmers who were growing white corn on farms located next to a creek. The pairing of white corn and soft West Virginia water offered the perfect combination to turn that corn into moonshine. Indeed, moonshine was the best cash crop that a West Virginia farmer ever had.

Unfortunately, Earl died young in 1925, in an era when women had little opportunity to enter into any workplace. Allie had to rely on her own creativity and ingenuity to keep a roof over her head and to put food on her table. Records show that she purchased a two-story house on Washington Street and opened her home to boarders. But Allie continued to work with the farmers—you know, to help sell and to distribute their moonshine.

Allie lived within sight of the State Capitol in downtown Charleston, so she had to keep a low profile and to behave herself as far as anyone could tell. She hired a 15-year-old lad to be a "look out." His duties included alerting Allie should someone arrive who was not invited, who should not be purchasing moonshine, or who was, heaven forbid, a "dang" revenuer nosing around. Allie had strict rules about selling to those who were underage or known to be "drunkards." As a moonshiner, she had her principles.

With some of her earnings, Allie bought a black 1925 Packard automobile—the big one. The young man drove her Packard to make deliveries after midnight. He had grown up in Kanawha County, so he knew all the back roads. He could easily navigate them under the cover of the darkness; the revenuers could not. No one suspected that he was making deliveries, but Allie often rode along in the passenger seat anyway. She knew that an automobile with a woman in it was not as likely to be stopped or searched by the authorities.

One day the sheriff came to greet Allie at the boarding house with a "Good afternoon, Mrs. Cavender." One might imagine that he was campaigning for re-election, but he was really signaling Allie to hide her moonshine. He had learned that a search warrant for her residence had been issued by the revenuers. The sheriff might well have been thinking about votes, but he was probably just as interested in getting a quart of moonshine in exchange for providing the information.

The revenuers came, just as expected. Allie had placed some quart jars of moonshine in an empty flour barrel. Then she sat on top of the barrel so that it was hidden beneath the flowing skirt of her long dress that touched the floor. Allie knew women were protected by laws from having their persons searched. Moreover, unknown to the revenuers, they were standing on a rug that concealed a trap door to more moonshine hidden under the floor. Disappointed in finding no illegal moonshine, the revenuers left Allie's home. Allie later boasted when telling that story, "I out-foxed those fellers."

Allie felt an obligation to use some of her earnings from the sale of the moonshine to provide for her family, friends, and those in the community "down on their luck." She is remembered for delivering big bags of groceries to Earl's relatives and her brother, Jeffrey, and his family on Sundays and holidays. Their children looked forward to rides in her Packard into the country when she came for a visit.

Allie Cavender died in 1946 in Charleston. It is said that quite a crowd attended her funeral, including several state officials and political leaders with whom she was acquainted. Some said that she was no more than a common outlaw. Others who knew her better called her a "hometown hero," someone who made life better for those around her. By all accounts, she was an independent woman of great strength, generosity, and resourcefulness. She did what she needed to survive.

And although some thought she had lost her way, I think they came to find out what the family already knew: Times were tough, but my great-grandmother Allie was tougher. •

Paula Teem Levi is a retired Registered Nurse living in Clover, South Carolina. She is a member of several genealogical societies. Her stories have appeared in six previous anthologies of the Personal Story Publishing Project. "Who's That Lady," which appeared in *Curious Stuff,* was recently published in the *Journal of the Burke County (NC) Genealogical Society.* Paula's goal is to preserve as many family stories as possible for future generations so that they will not be at risk of being forgotten or lost forever.

Uplifting Good Fortune
by Judie Holcomb-Pack

I find it exhilarating watching a Chinese take-out box taking flight when it's least expected, especially one large enough to fit inside the back of a pick-up truck. Until that time, I had never considered the aerodynamic design of a take-out box, how the open flaps form perfect wings to lift it up, to help it soar up and away.

Before I retired, I worked in marketing for a nonprofit organization in Winston-Salem, North Carolina. Part of my job involved planning special events, especially fundraisers. Just such an opportunity was presented to us when a local bank announced its grand opening of a new branch in a town close by. To generate interest and excitement, they planned to have a parade of "floats" through town to their new location and offered a top prize of $500 to a nonprofit group with the best designed float.

We accepted the challenge and immediately began to imagine a theme and create a design for our submission. As our nonprofit provided emergency assistance to our neighbors in need, we came up with the idea of how our financial support brought "good fortune" to those in crisis situations. And what better way to illustrate this concept than a fortune cookie! I found a promotional company that would insert our own "fortunes" inside cookies for a reasonable price. These would be handed out from our float along the parade route. What fun!

I persuaded a friend who worked in the promotional packaging industry to design a giant, oversized Chinese take-out box that would fit in the back of a pickup truck. Our financial manager volunteered his truck for us to use in the parade. Our teen volunteers would ride inside the take-out box and toss out our fortune cookies to parade watchers.

That $500 was as good as already deposited into our bank account, we thought. We had created a winning theme, design, and a unique giveaway item.

What could go wrong? What we never considered was aerodynamics.

Early that Saturday morning, we put the giant take-out box into the truck bed and weighed down the corners with boxes of fortune cookies and cartons of brochures. Our executive director took off down the street driving the truck and I followed in my car. Things were going well until she merged onto Business 40 and picked up speed. As we both approached 45 miles per hour, I watched in fascination as the flaps on the Chinese take-out box rose like airplane wings and the box took flight. It sailed out of the back of the truck and landed smoothly onto the interstate highway, no less impressively than Orville and Wilbur Wright at Kitty Hawk.

My co-worker immediately pulled over to the side of the road and I stopped behind her. Standing on the side of the 4-lane thoroughfare, watching early morning traffic run over our display, I could just see that $500 prize floating away into the clouds. But being an optimist, I looked at my co-worker and I said, "I think we can fix this." When we saw a break in the traffic, we dashed into the roadway and picked up pieces of the display and put them back into the truck. It was a little harrowing, but with $500 dangling in front of my eyes, I focused on the task at hand.

When we arrived at our destination where our teen volunteers were anxiously awaiting us, I quickly grabbed the event toolbox I kept in the trunk of my car. I pulled out a roll of duct tape and began repairing the giant take-out box. Surprisingly, it had withstood its flight from the truck and its highway landing, and although there were a few tire tracks along the sides, it was none the worse for wear.

We joined the parade and enjoyed seeing the smiles on children's faces when they caught the fortune cookies and read the message inside: "Good fortune comes when you help neighbors in need."

Later at the ribbon cutting, the bank official announced they were so impressed with the displays that EVERY nonprofit would receive a check for $500.

Sometime later I reflected on our challenging morning and how easily our mishap could have resulted in injury. I realized that at no time did we consider giving up. It never occurred to us to just dump the display and consider the prize money a loss. We were both focused on the goal of winning a donation to our nonprofit and felt confident we could succeed.

We almost lost our flying display, but we found lessons worth more than a $500 check, the real sources of "good fortune": ingenuity in creative problem solving, the power of focusing on a goal, the omnipotent utility of duct tape, and the universal laws of aerodynamics. •

After a career in public relations, marketing and special events, Judie Holcomb-Pack retired from a local nonprofit and immediately switched gears and became the assistant editor of a weekly newspaper for the African American community in Winston-Salem. She is a member of Winston-Salem Writers and writes poetry, short stories, essays, and ten-minute plays. She especially enjoys interviewing and writing about interesting older adults for The Chronicle's monthly section, "For Seniors Only."

GPS on the Blue Ridge Parkway

by David Winship

T he drive was to a mountain cabin off the Blue Ridge Parkway near Chateau Morrisette Winery to celebrate my 71st birthday. I'd driven from Bristol, Tennessee, to Winston-Salem, North Carolina, in the morning, on the interstate highways with the only interruption being patches of fog at Fancy Gap, Virginia.

In Winston-Salem, I picked up my girlfriend, and we headed to the mountains, a direct route on Highway 52 north through Mount Airy to Cana, Virginia, where we turned north on the Blue Ridge Parkway. It is about an hour drive to the parkway and about another 40 minutes to the destination, according to directions on Google Maps using GPS.

When we turned onto the Parkway, we immediately encountered a heavy fog, and we lost all cell phone service. We were not worried as we knew the winery was off the Parkway and my companion remembered that the winery was north of Mabry Mill, the landmark we would first recognize.

The fog was heavy, heavier than any I'd ever driven through. This was dense, bright white fog, which gave an element of winter wonderland to the surrounding forests and open spaces through which we were driving. The mistiness made it fairytale-like. The fog was heaviest on the ridges, where visibility would be about two car lengths.

With great effort, we scanned out the windows of each side of the car. My partner recalled memories of a sign and the winery's proximity to the parkway. On we drove, mile by mile, searching through the heavy fog. Driving between the right solid line and the mid-road broken line was the only way to guide the car down the road. Visibility beyond the car hood was fuzzy.

We passed a sign designating Meadows of Dan, which we knew to be the address of the winery, so we knew we were close. Then we passed an intersection which indicated that Floyd, which we knew to be a nearby town, was down the mountain. Still no sign of the winery.

We continued driving with increasing vigilance, knowing the sign was somewhere, somewhere obscured by the fog which was everywhere. Whereas the speed limit on the parkway is 45, creeping along at 25 seemed fast. Several times, the whiteness of the fog combined with the whiteness of a tail and a brown body as deer bounded across the road. We narrowly missed a few collisions. At other times, the red waddle of wild turkeys indicated they were in residence in the middle of the road. Still the fog shrouded our view beyond the roadway, like the opening scenes in an old black and white horror movie.

We entered that time in our journey when we knew we were on the right road, but we suspected we had gone too far, yet we hesitated to turn around for fear that our destination was just up around the bend. If that wasn't bad enough, the coffee we'd been drinking needed relief. We had passed many signs for overlooks and had commented that there would not be much to see on a day like this. So, the increased urgency for relief prompted us to stop at one when we could at least see the turnoff.

After a much-appreciated "pit stop," we discovered to our joy and relief that cell phone reception had returned to the high location. As if by magic, the map appeared with the route marked from our location to the address for the mountain cabin. The pleasant voice in English accent announced, "Return to route and go 30 miles." We were to backtrack the way we had just come.

Winding our way through the fog over a now-familiar road, we finally reached the cabin safely for our weekend stay. It was nestled in the fog, barely visible from the road, but very warm and welcoming inside.

As a society, we have come to a time where we no longer rely on verbal or written directions and folded maps are no longer at hand in the car. We depend on the GPS on our phones and expect to be taken directly to a destination, to where we want to go, or to where we are supposed to be. On this trip, however, we had a sense that there was some divine guidance

system in place on this trip, where the good Lord had determined that we had wandered long enough, perhaps not 40
years in the wilderness, but still, long enough. We were not
lost, really, we simply did not know where we were. We were
re-connected and re-directed to find our cabin in the
mountains by GPS—as we like to think of it—God's
Positioning System. •

David Winship lives in Bristol, Tennessee, and is a retired public-
school educator. Having returned to age out at his family homeplace,
he writes primarily concerning his sense of place in the natural
world. He publishes an annual chapbook of poetry and is a member
of the Appalachian Center for Poets and Writers and Winston-Salem
Writers.

(This story includes graphic descriptions of fatal injuries.)

It Was Not Her Fault
by Randell Jones

Somebody wanted a pound of flesh.

I heard the story in dribs and drabs over months during morning walks with my neighbor. He was approaching 90 and was still capable of walking around the neighborhood at a decent pace on a cool morning. The real tragedy unfolded slowly after the revelations in the first episode: his granddaughter had been in a bad car accident. Three of her friends were dead. She had survived by a miracle.

She was 19, out with friends in her mother's car celebrating her graduation from a certificate school in cosmetology. She picked up a fellow graduate and a couple the other girl knew better. They were out for the evening, but first made a stop to meet up with others. The parents at the second stop welcomed them in and offered the under-age celebrants drinks before they took off. The granddaughter was tiny, less than ninety pounds. Even a partial drink went straight to her head.

The celebrants soon left in two cars headed for a house party a few miles away. Challenges were made, last-one-there-is-a-loser sort of thing. Her car took off like a rocket, the others watching its taillights disappear ahead. But in the darkness of the rural road with houses well off the blacktop, those in the following car soon saw a flash of taillights, headlights, taillights, headlights. The granddaughter's car was out of control, spinning around, and careening out of sight downhill and into the woods.

Those behind arrived on the scene in a matter of seconds. They ran down to find the granddaughter's car slammed into a tree, the car cracked open like an egg. What they saw was horrible. The female front-seat passenger had been shoved into the rear of the car by a tree limb coming through the windshield, impaling her. The female previously seated behind her was later found dead by the road, catapulted from the vehicle when it first began to spin. The granddaughter was soon found unconscious but alive on the ground near the car, apparently ejected before impact. The boyfriend of the front-seat passenger was dead inside the vehicle draped across the console with his skull cracked open. The windshield was shattered from the inside and human brain tissue was on the car's dash. His upper torso had crushing injuries consistent with striking a steering wheel.

When the first responders arrived on scene, some of them knew the dead male; they were friends. By the time the State Trooper arrived, someone had shoveled mud and grass onto the car's dash. The Trooper later identified the car as belonging to the granddaughter's mother. He listed the hospitalized granddaughter, the sole survivor, as the car's driver.

The wrecked car was hauled away to the county's impound lot and left outside in the elements for weeks as an investigation began. The investigators talked to the parents who had given the underage celebrants drinks. Their daughter had been in the other car. The two parents corroborated whatever the investigators wanted to conclude; no charges were filed against them.

The grandfather hired a forensic investigator who modeled the dynamics of the crash, calculating the forces involved, knowing the positions of bodies afterward. He concluded that the male was the likely driver, and that the granddaughter was most probably in the backseat behind the driver, passed out from the effects of the alcohol, all of which would have enhanced her chances of survival.

The assistant district attorney, recently recognized by an anti-drunk-driving organization for her diligent work, charged the granddaughter with what the grandfather simply called "murder." The judge, on loan from a neighboring county, had a reputation as a "hanging judge"—short on compassion, big on consequences. Wanting a conviction, the prosecutor offered an Alford Plea. The granddaughter would not have to admit guilt, just agree to accept the sentence for manslaughter knowing that the prosecutor had, they believed, enough evidence to get a guilty verdict at trial—40 years for murder, the grandfather said.

At the sentencing, the families of the deceased showed photo albums to the judge as they grieved publicly over the loss of their young adult children taken from them just as their lives were beginning. The granddaughter sobbed and wept on the stand, apologizing profusely for whatever she had done. She did not remember anything, nothing after a drink at the house of somebody's parents. She was sentenced to seven years in prison.

Even the warden noticed something was wrong. The granddaughter was not like the other inmates. She did not belong there. She could get early release if she participated in a special program for felons, but to qualify, she would have to admit guilt. She refused. She served out her full sentence.

When she was released, having lost seven years of her 20s, she could not hug her grandfather., but it was not her fault. We had buried him two years before. •

Randell Jones is an award-winning writer about the pioneer and Revolutionary War eras and North Carolina history. During 25 years, he has written 100+ history-based guest columns for the Winston-Salem Journal. In 2017, he created the Personal Story Publishing Project and in 2019, the companion podcast, "6-minute Stories" to encourage other writers. He lives in Winston-Salem, North Carolina. Visit BecomingAmerica250.com and RandellJones.com.

Randell promised the grandfather several years ago that he would write this story. Rest in peace.